CARLOS CARL

FLORIDA STATE PARKS GUIDE

Copyright © 2024 by CARLOS CARL

All rights reserved. No part of this publication may be reproduced, stored or transmitted in any form or by any means, electronic, mechanical, photocopying, recording, scanning, or otherwise without written permission from the publisher. It is illegal to copy this book, post it to a website, or distribute it by any other means without permission.

First edition

*This book was professionally typeset on Reedsy.
Find out more at reedsy.com*

Contents

Introduction	1
WELCOME TO FLORIDA STATE PARKS	1
A Brief History of Florida State Parks	2
Conservation Efforts and Wildlife Protection	5
1 Chapter 1	11
NORTHERN FLORIDA STATE PARKS	11
Blackwater River State Park	12
Big Lagoon State Park	15
Falling Waters State Park	19
Florida Caverns State Park	22
Outdoor Activities and Adventures	26
Accommodation Options In Northern Florida	29
Local Flora and Fauna of Northern Florida	34
2 Chapter 2	40
CENTRAL FLORIDA STATE PARKS	40
Wekiwa Springs State Park	42
Blue Spring State Park	46
De Leon Springs State Park	49
Lake Louisa State Park	53
Outdoor Activities and Adventures	56
Accommodation Options In Central Florida	60
Local Flora and Fauna	64
3 Chapter 3	68

SOUTHERN FLORIDA	68
John Pennekamp Coral Reef State Park	69
Everglades National Park	72
Oleta River State Park	75
Bahia Honda State Park	78
Outdoor Activities and Adventures	81
Accommodation Options in Southern Florida	86
Local Flora and Fauna	91
4 Chapter 4	96
COASTAL FLORIDA	96
Honeymoon Island State Park	98
Caladesi Island State Park	101
Sebastian Inlet State Park	105
Accommodation Options In Coastal Florida	110
5 Chapter 5	116
SPECIAL INTEREST PARKS	116
Historical Parks	117
Botanical Gardens	121
Birdwatching Spots	124
Scenic Drives and Hiking Trails	128
6 Chapter 6	132
CULINARY OPTIONS	132
Picnic Areas and Facilities	133
On-site Cafes and Restaurants	136
Local Cuisine and Food Festivals	140
Cooking in the Wild: Campfire Recipes and Tips	143
7 Chapter 7	146
PRACTICAL INFORMATION	146
Park Passes and Fees	147

    Accessibility Information   149
    Safety Tips and Regulations   153
    Packing Lists and Gear Recommendations.   156
8 Conclusion   160

Introduction

WELCOME TO FLORIDA STATE PARKS

Welcome to Florida State Parks, a world where natural beauty, rich history, and diverse wildlife come together to create an unparalleled outdoor experience. Florida's state parks offer a unique glimpse into the state's varied ecosystems, from the pristine beaches of the Gulf and Atlantic coasts to the dense forests and tranquil rivers of the interior. Whether you are an avid hiker, a water sports enthusiast, a history buff, or simply someone looking to unwind in nature, Florida's state parks have something for everyone. These parks are not just destinations; they are sanctuaries for endangered species, living museums of the state's cultural heritage, and playgrounds for adventure seekers. The Florida State Parks system is a testament to the state's commitment to preserving its natural treasures for future generations. With over 175 parks spanning nearly 800,000 acres, there are endless opportunities for exploration and discovery. Visitors can enjoy a range of activities, including kayaking through mangrove tunnels, snorkeling in crystal-clear springs, camping under starlit skies, or exploring historic forts. Each park tells its own story, from the ancient Native American mounds at Crystal River Archaeological State Park to the underwater wonders of John Pennekamp Coral Reef State

Park. As you embark on your journey through these pages, prepare to be inspired by the breathtaking landscapes and vibrant ecosystems that make Florida State Parks a true natural wonder.

A Brief History of Florida State Parks

The history of Florida State Parks is a rich tapestry woven with the threads of conservation, recreation, and cultural preservation. Here's a detailed account of the key milestones and developments:

Early 20th Century: Beginnings of Conservation

- **1920s**: The movement to preserve Florida's natural landscapes began gaining momentum. Public interest in conservation was spurred by the rapid development and exploitation of natural resources.
- **1927**: The Florida Board of Forestry was created, marking the state's first official recognition of the need for forest and land conservation.

1930s: Establishment of the First State Parks

- **1931**: Florida's first state park, Myakka River State Park, was established. Located near Sarasota, Myakka River set the precedent for future state parks in terms of land preservation and public recreation.
- **1933**: The Civilian Conservation Corps (CCC), a New Deal

program, played a crucial role in developing many of Florida's early state parks. The CCC built facilities, trails, and infrastructure that are still in use today.
- **1935**: Florida Caverns State Park was established, becoming the only state park in Florida to offer cave tours to the public.

1940s-1950s: Expansion and Development

- **1949**: The Florida Park Service was formally established, tasked with managing and expanding the state park system. The same year, Hugh Taylor Birch State Park was established in Fort Lauderdale.
- **1950s**: The state park system continued to grow, with a focus on acquiring and preserving diverse ecosystems, from coastal areas to inland forests. Parks like Highlands Hammock State Park (1952) and John Pennekamp Coral Reef State Park (1959) were added.

1960s-1970s: Environmental Awareness and Growth

- **1963**: The Outdoor Recreation and Conservation Act was passed, providing funding and a legal framework for the expansion and maintenance of state parks.
- **1969**: The Environmental Protection Act further solidified Florida's commitment to environmental preservation. During this period, the state park system saw significant growth, with many new parks established.
- **1970**: Paynes Prairie Preserve State Park was established, recognized for its unique grassland ecosystem and historical significance.

1980s-1990s: Modernization and Preservation

- **1985**: The Save Our Rivers program was initiated to protect water resources through land acquisition, benefiting many state parks located near rivers and springs.
- **1990s**: Florida continued to prioritize environmental preservation. The Preservation 2000 Act, passed in 1990, allocated funds for acquiring and preserving natural lands, enhancing the state park system.

2000s-Present: Continued Growth and Innovation

- **2000**: The Florida Forever program succeeded Preservation 2000, continuing the state's efforts to protect critical lands and waterways. This program has been instrumental in expanding the state park system.
- **2010**: The Florida Park Service celebrated its 75th anniversary, reflecting on decades of growth and achievement in conservation and public recreation.
- **2016**: St. Joseph Peninsula State Park was named the top beach in America by Dr. Beach, highlighting the natural beauty and recreational appeal of Florida's state parks.
- **2020s**: The state park system continues to innovate and adapt, incorporating sustainability practices, enhancing visitor facilities, and expanding educational programs to foster environmental stewardship.

Key Themes in Florida State Parks History

- **Conservation**: From the early days of Myakka River State Park to the modern Florida Forever program, conservation

has always been a cornerstone of Florida's state park system.
- **Public Recreation**: The development of trails, campgrounds, and visitor centers has made the parks accessible and enjoyable for millions of visitors each year.
- **Cultural Preservation**: Many state parks protect and interpret significant historical and archaeological sites, preserving Florida's rich cultural heritage for future generations.

Florida's state parks are a testament to the state's enduring commitment to preserving its natural and cultural treasures. Today, the Florida State Parks system comprises over 175 parks, covering nearly 800,000 acres of diverse landscapes, providing countless opportunities for recreation, education, and inspiration.

Conservation Efforts and Wildlife Protection

Florida State Parks are renowned for their exceptional efforts in conservation and wildlife protection. These efforts are critical for maintaining the state's diverse ecosystems, safeguarding endangered species, and ensuring the natural beauty of Florida for future generations. Here's a detailed look at the various initiatives and programs in place:

Habitat Restoration and Management

1. **Prescribed Burns**

- Prescribed burns are controlled fires used to manage ecosystems that depend on periodic fire for regeneration and health. Florida's ecosystems, such as pine flatwoods and scrub habitats, benefit from these burns, which reduce invasive species, recycle nutrients, and promote the growth of native plants.

1. **Invasive Species Control**

- Invasive species, both plant and animal, pose significant threats to native ecosystems. Florida State Parks engage in active monitoring and removal of invasive species, such as Brazilian pepper and air potato, to restore native habitats and protect biodiversity.

1. **Wetland Restoration**

- Wetlands are vital for water purification, flood control, and providing habitat for numerous species. Restoration projects often involve reestablishing natural water flow, removing invasive plants, and planting native vegetation. Examples include the restoration efforts at Wekiwa Springs State Park and the Everglades.

Species Protection Programs

1. **Endangered and Threatened Species**

- Florida State Parks serve as refuges for many endangered and threatened species, including the Florida panther, manatee, and various sea turtles. Parks implement specific management plans tailored to the needs of these species, such as protecting nesting sites, monitoring populations, and reducing human-wildlife conflicts.

1. **Wildlife Corridors**

- Establishing wildlife corridors ensures that animals can move freely between habitats, which is crucial for genetic diversity and species survival. Florida State Parks collaborate with other agencies and organizations to create and maintain these corridors, facilitating the safe passage of wildlife.

Education and Outreach

1. **Environmental Education Programs**

- Parks offer educational programs and interpretive exhibits to raise awareness about conservation issues and the importance of protecting natural resources. These programs target school groups, local communities, and park visitors, fostering a deeper understanding and appreciation of Florida's ecosystems.

1. **Citizen Science Initiatives**

- Engaging the public in conservation efforts is a key strategy. Citizen science programs invite volunteers to participate in activities like bird counts, water quality monitoring, and plant surveys. This not only aids in data collection but also enhances public involvement and stewardship.

Sustainable Practices

1. Eco-friendly Facilities

- Many state parks have implemented sustainable practices in their facilities, such as using solar power, recycling programs, and water conservation measures. These practices reduce the environmental footprint of park operations and set an example for visitors.

1. Green Certifications

- Several Florida State Parks have received green certifications for their sustainable practices, highlighting their commitment to environmental responsibility. These certifications often involve rigorous assessments of energy use, waste management, and conservation efforts.

Partnerships and Collaborations

1. Interagency Cooperation

- Florida State Parks work closely with other state and federal agencies, such as the Florida Fish and Wildlife Conservation Commission and the U.S. Fish and Wildlife Service, to align conservation efforts and share resources and expertise.

1. Nonprofit and Community Involvement

- Partnerships with nonprofit organizations, such as the Florida State Parks Foundation, provide additional support for conservation projects. Community involvement is also encouraged through volunteer programs and local conservation initiatives.

Research and Monitoring

1. **Scientific Research**

- Ongoing scientific research within state parks helps inform management practices and conservation strategies. Studies on species behavior, habitat requirements, and environmental changes provide valuable data for adaptive management.

1. **Long-term Monitoring**

- Long-term ecological monitoring programs track the health of ecosystems and the success of conservation efforts. Data from these programs guide management decisions and help detect emerging threats, such as climate change impacts or new invasive species.

Success Stories

1. **Manatee Protection**

- Blue Spring State Park is a success story in manatee conservation. The park provides a winter refuge for manatees, and efforts to protect these gentle giants have led to significant increases in their population.

1. **Sea Turtle Conservation**

- At parks like John Pennekamp Coral Reef State Park and Sebastian Inlet State Park, dedicated efforts to protect sea turtle nesting sites have resulted in higher hatchling success rates and increased public awareness about the importance of protecting these ancient mariners.

Through these comprehensive conservation efforts and wildlife protection programs, Florida State Parks not only preserve the state's natural heritage but also promote sustainable practices and foster a culture of environmental stewardship. These efforts ensure that Florida's unique ecosystems and wildlife will continue to thrive for generations to come.

1

Chapter 1

NORTHERN FLORIDA STATE PARKS

Northern Florida is a region of diverse landscapes, rich history, and abundant natural beauty. Stretching from the rolling hills of the Panhandle to the serene coastal areas along the Gulf of Mexico and the Atlantic Ocean, this area is a haven for outdoor enthusiasts and nature lovers. The region is characterized by its lush forests, pristine rivers, and unspoiled beaches, offering a tranquil escape from the hustle and bustle of urban life. Northern Florida is home to some of the state's most iconic state parks, such as Blackwater River State Park, known for its crystal-clear waters and canoeing opportunities, and Florida Caverns State Park, which offers a rare glimpse into Florida's subterranean wonders with its intricate limestone caves. The region's mild climate makes it a year-round destination for hiking, camping, fishing, and wildlife watching. Additionally, Northern Florida is steeped in history, with numerous parks preserving the remnants of early

Native American civilizations, colonial settlements, and Civil War battlefields. Visitors can explore the ancient mounds at Crystal River Archaeological State Park or step back in time at Olustee Battlefield Historic State Park. With its combination of natural beauty and historical significance, Northern Florida provides a captivating experience for all who visit, making it an essential part of any Florida State Parks adventure.

Blackwater River State Park

Blackwater River State Park, located in the western panhandle of Florida, is renowned for its stunning natural beauty and crystal-clear river. Established in 1967, the park protects a significant portion of the Blackwater River, one of the purest sand-bottom rivers in the nation. The park's name derives from the dark tannic waters of the river, which contrast beautifully with the white sandy banks and lush green forests. The park's history is intertwined with the development of the region, from Native American settlements to early European exploration and subsequent logging activities that once dominated the area. Today, Blackwater River State Park serves as a sanctuary for outdoor recreation and conservation, offering visitors a glimpse into Florida's natural heritage.

Location

Blackwater River State Park is located at: 7720 Deaton Bridge Road, Holt, FL 32564

The park is easily accessible from Interstate 10, making it a convenient destination for both locals and travelers.

Main Attractions

- **Blackwater River**: The park's centerpiece, offering opportunities for canoeing, kayaking, and tubing in its clear, cool waters.
- **White Sand Beaches**: Ideal for picnicking and relaxation along the riverbanks.
- **Nature Trails**: Several hiking trails wind through the park, showcasing its diverse ecosystems and providing excellent wildlife viewing opportunities.

Prices

- **Entrance Fee**: $4 per vehicle (single-occupant), $5 per vehicle (2-8 occupants), and $2 per pedestrian or bicyclist.
- **Camping Fees**: Approximately $20 per night for a campsite with electric and water hookups.

Activities

- **Canoeing/Kayaking**: The Blackwater River offers a serene paddling experience, with the river stretching over 31 miles in total.
- **Hiking**: The Juniper Lake Trail and other trails offer scenic views and a chance to explore the park's diverse flora and fauna.
- **Fishing**: Anglers can enjoy fishing in the river, with opportunities to catch bass, bream, and catfish.
- **Swimming and Tubing**: The park's sandy beaches and

shallow waters are perfect for swimming and tubing.
- **Picnicking**: Numerous picnic areas are available, equipped with tables and grills.

Facilities

- **Campgrounds**: The park features a well-maintained campground with 30 campsites, each equipped with water and electric hookups.
- **Restrooms and Showers**: Clean and accessible restrooms and shower facilities are available for campers and day visitors.
- **Picnic Areas**: Multiple picnic pavilions and individual picnic spots with tables and grills.
- **Boat Ramp**: A convenient launch site for canoes and kayaks.
- **Nature Center**: Provides educational exhibits about the park's natural and cultural history.

Visitor Tips

- **Plan Ahead**: Reserve campsites in advance, especially during peak seasons.
- **Stay Hydrated**: Bring plenty of water, especially during hot summer months.
- **Protect Yourself from the Sun**: Wear sunscreen, hats, and sunglasses.
- **Bug Spray**: Insect repellent is recommended to ward off mosquitoes and ticks.
- **Respect Wildlife**: Observe animals from a distance and do not feed them.
- **Leave No Trace**: Pack out all trash and leave the park as

pristine as you found it.
- **Safety First**: Always wear a life jacket when canoeing or kayaking and be aware of river currents and weather conditions.
- **Explore Beyond the River**: Take time to hike the trails and explore the different habitats within the park.

Blackwater River State Park offers a serene escape into nature with a variety of activities and facilities that cater to all kinds of outdoor enthusiasts. Whether you're paddling down the river, hiking through the forest, or simply relaxing on a sandy beach, the park provides a memorable experience in the heart of Florida's panhandle.

Big Lagoon State Park

Big Lagoon State Park, located near Pensacola in Escambia County, Florida, is a gem of the Gulf Coast, offering diverse ecosystems that include saltwater marshes, pine flatwoods, and sandy beaches. Established in 1978, the park spans over 705 acres and serves as a crucial barrier between the mainland and Perdido Key, an important area for wildlife and migratory birds. Its establishment aimed to protect these vital habitats while providing recreational opportunities for visitors. The park's name derives from the large lagoon that forms part of the Intracoastal Waterway, which provides an array of water-based activities and stunning natural scenery.

Location

Big Lagoon State Park is located at: 12301 Gulf Beach Highway, Pensacola, FL 32507

The park is easily accessible via Highway 292 and is just a short drive from downtown Pensacola.

Main Attractions

- **Observation Tower**: A five-story tower offering panoramic views of the park, the Gulf of Mexico, and Perdido Key.
- **West Beach**: A sandy beach area perfect for sunbathing, swimming, and beachcombing.
- **Bird Watching**: The park is part of the Great Florida Birding Trail, attracting birdwatchers with its diverse avian population.

Prices

- **Entrance Fee**: $6 per vehicle (2-8 occupants), $4 for single-occupant vehicles, and $2 for pedestrians or bicyclists.
- **Camping Fees**: Approximately $20-$30 per night for a campsite with electric and water hookups.

Activities

- **Canoeing/Kayaking**: The park's waterways and lagoon provide excellent paddling opportunities. Canoe and kayak rentals are available.
- **Fishing**: Popular spots include the Long Pond and the Intracoastal Waterway, where anglers can catch redfish, flounder, and speckled trout.

- **Swimming**: Designated swimming areas are available for safe enjoyment of the lagoon's waters.
- **Bird Watching**: With more than 200 species recorded, the park is a birdwatcher's paradise, especially during migration seasons.
- **Hiking and Biking**: The park features several trails that wind through its diverse habitats, offering both hiking and biking opportunities.

Facilities

- **Campgrounds**: The park has 75 campsites, all with electric and water hookups, as well as nearby restrooms with showers.
- **Picnic Areas**: Equipped with tables, grills, and pavilions, perfect for family gatherings and group outings.
- **Boat Ramp**: Provides access to the Intracoastal Waterway and Big Lagoon for boaters and anglers.
- **Restrooms and Showers**: Clean and accessible facilities are available throughout the park.
- **Observation Tower**: Offers stunning views and photo opportunities.

Trails and Activities

- **Sand Pine Trail**: A 2-mile loop trail through pine flatwoods, ideal for hiking and birdwatching.
- **Estuary Trail**: A 1.9-mile trail along the lagoon, offering views of salt marshes and opportunities to spot wildlife.
- **Perdido Bay Trail**: A 2.3-mile trail that provides a scenic walk through various ecosystems, perfect for both hiking

and biking.
- **Paddle Trails**: Marked water trails for canoeing and kayaking, with varying lengths and difficulty levels.

Visitor Tips

- **Plan Ahead**: Reserve campsites and check for any park alerts or weather conditions.
- **Bring Essentials**: Sunscreen, bug spray, and plenty of water are crucial for a comfortable visit.
- **Wildlife Awareness**: Keep a respectful distance from wildlife and avoid feeding animals.
- **Leave No Trace**: Follow the principles of Leave No Trace to help preserve the park's natural beauty.
- **Safety First**: Always wear a life jacket when on the water and be aware of changing tides and weather conditions.
- **Stay on Trails**: Stick to designated trails to protect the environment and for your safety.
- **Early Bird Watching**: For bird enthusiasts, early morning is the best time to see the most activity.
- **Photography**: Don't forget your camera, especially for capturing the views from the observation tower and the abundant wildlife.

Big Lagoon State Park offers a unique blend of coastal beauty, recreational activities, and wildlife observation opportunities. Whether you're paddling through the lagoon, hiking through pine forests, or simply enjoying a picnic by the water, the park provides a serene and enriching experience in the heart of Florida's Gulf Coast.

Falling Waters State Park

Falling Waters State Park, located in the Florida Panhandle, is a natural wonder known for its impressive waterfall, the tallest in Florida. Established in 1962, the park encompasses a variety of geological features, including sinkholes, caves, and a scenic lake. The centerpiece of the park is Falling Waters Sink, where a stream cascades 73 feet into a cylindrical sinkhole before disappearing into a cave system. The park's history is rich, with evidence of Native American habitation and early European settlers who utilized the area's natural resources. The park was officially developed to protect these unique geological features and provide recreational opportunities for visitors.

Location

Falling Waters State Park is located at: 1130 State Park Road, Chipley, FL 32428

The park is accessible via Interstate 10, making it an easy destination for travelers.

Main Attractions

- **Falling Waters Sink**: The 73-foot waterfall is the tallest in Florida, plunging into a sinkhole with a captivating view.
- **Sinkholes and Caves**: The park features numerous sinkholes and a cave system, providing a glimpse into Florida's geological past.
- **Falling Waters Lake**: A serene lake offering opportunities for fishing and picnicking.

Prices

- **Entrance Fee**: $5 per vehicle (2-8 occupants), $4 for single-occupant vehicles, and $2 for pedestrians or bicyclists.
- **Camping Fees**: Approximately $18 per night for a campsite with electric and water hookups.

Activities

- **Hiking**: The park's trails offer scenic views and access to various natural features, including the waterfall and sinkholes.
- **Bird Watching**: The park is home to a variety of bird species, making it a great spot for bird enthusiasts.
- **Picnicking**: Several picnic areas are available with tables and grills, perfect for family outings.
- **Fishing**: The lake is stocked with fish, providing a peaceful fishing experience.
- **Swimming**: A designated swimming area in the lake is available for visitors to enjoy.

Measurements/Height

- **Falling Waters Sink**: The waterfall drops 73 feet into a cylindrical sinkhole, making it the tallest waterfall in Florida.

Facilities

- **Campgrounds**: The park offers 24 campsites, each equipped with water and electric hookups, picnic tables, and grills.
- **Restrooms and Showers**: Clean and accessible facilities are

available for campers and day visitors.
- **Picnic Areas**: Multiple areas with tables and grills, and a pavilion that can be reserved for group events.
- **Playground**: A playground is available for children to enjoy.
- **Visitor Center**: Provides information about the park's natural features and history.

Trails and Activities

- **Sinkhole Trail**: A 1.3-mile trail that leads to the waterfall and other sinkholes, providing scenic views and interpretive signage about the park's geology.
- **Wiregrass Trail**: A 0.75-mile trail that winds through pine forests and offers opportunities for wildlife viewing and bird watching.
- **Swimming Area**: A designated swimming area in Falling Waters Lake allows for safe and enjoyable water activities.
- **Fishing Spots**: Designated fishing areas along the lake offer a peaceful angling experience.

Visitor Tips

- **Plan Ahead**: Check the weather and park alerts before your visit, especially since heavy rains can affect the waterfall flow.
- **Bring Essentials**: Sunscreen, insect repellent, and plenty of water are crucial for a comfortable visit.
- **Stay on Trails**: Stick to marked trails to protect the environment and for your safety.
- **Respect Wildlife**: Observe animals from a distance and do not feed them.

- **Leave No Trace**: Follow the principles of Leave No Trace to help preserve the park's natural beauty.
- **Early Arrival**: Arriving early ensures you can enjoy the park with fewer crowds and better opportunities for wildlife observation.
- **Photography**: The waterfall and sinkholes provide excellent photo opportunities, so don't forget your camera.
- **Camping Reservations**: Campsites can fill up quickly, so it's best to reserve your spot in advance.

Falling Waters State Park offers a unique blend of geological wonders, serene landscapes, and recreational activities. Whether you're marveling at the waterfall, hiking through diverse habitats, or enjoying a picnic by the lake, the park provides a memorable and enriching outdoor experience in the Florida Panhandle.

Florida Caverns State Park

Florida Caverns State Park, located in the Florida Panhandle near the city of Marianna, is a unique destination offering a rare glimpse into the state's subterranean wonders. Established in 1942, the park is famous for its stunning limestone caves, which feature intricate stalactites, stalagmites, flowstones, and other fascinating formations. These caverns were formed over millions of years through the dissolution of limestone by acidic groundwater, creating a complex network of underground passages. Above ground, the park encompasses 1,319 acres of beautiful hardwood forests, springs, and the Chipola River, providing diverse recreational opportunities.

Activities

- **Cave Tours**: Guided tours of the caverns are the park's main attraction. These tours take visitors through a series of rooms and passageways, showcasing spectacular formations and offering insights into the geological history of the region. The tours last about 45 minutes and are suitable for all ages.
- **Hiking and Biking**: The park offers several trails that wind through its diverse landscapes, providing opportunities for both hiking and biking. Trails range from easy to moderate in difficulty.
- **Fishing and Boating**: The Chipola River and Blue Hole Spring are popular spots for fishing, where anglers can catch bass, catfish, and bream. Canoeing and kayaking are also popular activities on the river.
- **Picnicking**: Numerous picnic areas equipped with tables and grills are scattered throughout the park, perfect for family gatherings and relaxation.
- **Camping**: The park features a well-maintained campground with sites for tents and RVs, including amenities such as water and electric hookups, restrooms, and showers.

Trails

- **Bluff Trail**: This 1.2-mile loop trail offers scenic views of the Chipola River floodplain and passes through dense hardwood forests. It provides a moderate hike with some elevation changes.

- **Beaver Dam Trail**: A 0.9-mile trail that takes visitors through wetland areas and past a beaver dam, offering opportunities to observe wildlife and unique plant species.
- **Tunnel Cave Trail**: This 0.7-mile trail leads to the entrance of a smaller, non-commercial cave that can be explored with proper equipment and permits. The trail provides a moderate hike with some uneven terrain.
- **Upper Chipola River Greenway Trail**: A longer trail that extends beyond the park boundaries, ideal for more adventurous hikers and bikers looking to explore the river's surroundings.

Points of Interest

- **The Caverns**: The main highlight of the park, featuring rooms such as the Wedding Room, which is adorned with columns and flowstones, and the Soda Straw Room, known for its delicate, straw-like formations.
- **Blue Hole Spring**: A beautiful, crystal-clear spring that feeds into the Chipola River, offering a refreshing spot for swimming and snorkeling.
- **Visitor Center**: Provides educational exhibits about the park's natural and cultural history, including displays about the formation of the caverns and the flora and fauna of the area.
- **Historic Civilian Conservation Corps Structures**: The park features several structures built by the CCC in the 1930s, including a visitor center and picnic pavilions, showcasing the craftsmanship and history of this important New Deal program.

Nearby Attractions

- **Falling Waters State Park**: Located about 20 miles south of Florida Caverns State Park, this park features the tallest waterfall in Florida and offers hiking, camping, and picnicking opportunities.
- **Three Rivers State Park**: Situated near the Georgia border, this park offers boating, fishing, and camping along the shores of Lake Seminole, about 40 miles northeast of Florida Caverns.
- **Marianna**: The nearby city of Marianna offers additional amenities, including restaurants, shops, and historical sites such as the Battle of Marianna monument and the Joseph W. Russ Jr. House, a beautifully preserved Victorian-era home.
- **Chipola River Paddling Trail**: This designated paddling trail offers a scenic and leisurely way to explore the Chipola River, with multiple access points and opportunities to observe wildlife and natural beauty along the way.
- **Florida Caverns Golf Course**: An 18-hole golf course adjacent to the park, providing a scenic and challenging game for golf enthusiasts.

Florida Caverns State Park is a remarkable destination that combines geological wonders with diverse outdoor activities. Whether you're exploring the underground caverns, hiking through lush forests, or enjoying a peaceful day on the river, the park offers a unique and enriching experience for visitors of all ages.

Outdoor Activities and Adventures

Northern Florida, with its diverse landscapes ranging from pristine beaches to dense forests and rolling hills, offers a plethora of outdoor activities and adventures for nature enthusiasts and thrill-seekers alike. Here's a detailed look at some of the best outdoor experiences you can enjoy in this region:

1. **Hiking and Backpacking**

   - **Apalachicola National Forest**: Spanning over 632,890 acres, this is the largest national forest in Florida. It offers numerous trails, including the popular Florida National Scenic Trail, which provides a mix of pine flatwoods, swamps, and hardwood forests.
   - **Torreya State Park**: Known for its unique topography and rare species of plants and animals, the park offers challenging hiking trails with scenic views of the Apalachicola River. The 7.5-mile Torreya Hiking Trail is a favorite among backpackers.

2. **Camping**

   - **Ochlockonee River State Park**: Offers a serene camping experience with well-equipped campsites, surrounded by pine forests and located along the riverbank. It's perfect for tent and RV camping.
   - **Big Lagoon State Park**: Provides diverse camping options with sites featuring water and electric hookups. The park is close to the beach, offering a mix of terrestrial and aquatic adventures.

3. **Kayaking and Canoeing**

- **Suwannee River**: A famed paddling destination, the Suwannee River offers calm, scenic stretches perfect for canoeing and kayaking. Several outfitters provide rentals and guided tours.
- **Blackwater River**: Known for its clear, tannin-stained waters and white sandy beaches, the Blackwater River is ideal for a relaxing canoe or kayak trip. It's one of the purest sand-bottom rivers in the world.

4. **Fishing**

- **St. Marks National Wildlife Refuge**: This area is rich in diverse fish species, including redfish, speckled trout, and flounder. It's a popular spot for both freshwater and saltwater fishing.
- **Lake Talquin**: Created by the damming of the Ochlockonee River, this lake is renowned for its largemouth bass, crappie, and bream fishing opportunities.

5. **Bird Watching**

- **St. Marks National Wildlife Refuge**: A critical habitat for migratory birds, this refuge offers birdwatchers a chance to see species like the red-cockaded woodpecker, bald eagles, and various waterfowl.
- **Paynes Prairie Preserve State Park**: This park is designated as a National Natural Landmark and provides habitats for over 270 species of birds. Observation platforms and trails make birdwatching accessible and enjoyable.

6. Cycling

- **Gainesville-Hawthorne State Trail**: A 16-mile trail that runs through Paynes Prairie Preserve State Park, offering scenic views and a smooth path ideal for cyclists of all levels.
- **Blackwater Heritage State Trail**: This 8.1-mile paved trail starts in Milton and winds through the scenic countryside, providing a peaceful ride for cyclists.

7. Scuba Diving and Snorkeling

- **Devil's Den**: An underground spring in Williston, offering a unique diving experience with clear waters and prehistoric fossils embedded in the cave walls.
- **Wakulla Springs**: One of the world's largest and deepest freshwater springs, it offers excellent snorkeling and diving opportunities with a chance to see manatees and other aquatic wildlife.

8. Wildlife Viewing

- **Ichetucknee Springs State Park**: Famous for its crystal-clear springs and river, the park is home to a variety of wildlife, including river otters, turtles, and birds. The Ichetucknee River offers tubing and snorkeling adventures.
- **Apalachicola National Estuarine Research Reserve**: Provides opportunities to see diverse marine life and coastal wildlife, with educational programs and guided tours available.

9. Horseback Riding

- **Torreya State Park**: Offers several equestrian trails through its rugged landscape, providing a unique way to explore the park's natural beauty.
- **Florida Caverns State Park**: Besides its famous caves, the park features horseback riding trails that wind through scenic woodlands and along riverbanks.

10. **Zip-lining and Aerial Adventures**

- **Tallahassee Museum Tree-to-Tree Adventures**: Offers zip-lining courses and aerial obstacle courses for all skill levels, set in a beautiful natural environment.
- **The Canyons Zip Line and Canopy Tours**: Located near Ocala, this adventure park provides exhilarating zip-line courses over canyons and lakes, offering stunning views and adrenaline-pumping fun.

Northern Florida's diverse ecosystems and landscapes make it a paradise for outdoor enthusiasts. Whether you prefer a tranquil hike through old-growth forests, an exhilarating paddle down a winding river, or a relaxing day fishing on a serene lake, Northern Florida offers countless opportunities to connect with nature and enjoy the great outdoors.

Accommodation Options In Northern Florida

1. Torreya State Park

- **Location**: 2576 NW Torreya Park Rd, Bristol, FL 32321

- **Prices**: Campsites range from $16 to $18 per night. Cabins are available at approximately $40 per night.
- **Side Attractions**: The park offers scenic views of the Apalachicola River, challenging hiking trails, and historic Gregory House.
- **Visitor Tips**:
- **Reservations**: Book campsites and cabins in advance, especially during peak seasons.
- **Hiking Gear**: Bring sturdy shoes for the park's rugged terrain.
- **Wildlife**: Early mornings and late afternoons are the best times for wildlife viewing.

2. **Big Lagoon State Park**

- **Location**: 12301 Gulf Beach Highway, Pensacola, FL 32507
- **Prices**: Campsites with water and electric hookups are around $20-$30 per night.
- **Side Attractions**: Proximity to Perdido Key beaches, observation tower with panoramic views, birdwatching trails.
- **Visitor Tips**:
- **Sun Protection**: Bring sunscreen, hats, and sunglasses.
- **Kayak Rentals**: Available in the park; consider exploring the water trails.
- **Birding**: Bring binoculars for excellent birdwatching opportunities.

3. **Florida Caverns State Park**

- **Location**: 3345 Caverns Rd, Marianna, FL 32446
- **Prices**: Campsites range from $18 to $25 per night.

- **Side Attractions**: Guided cave tours, Blue Hole Spring, Chipola River paddling.
- **Visitor Tips**:
- **Cave Tours**: Book tours early, as they can fill up quickly.
- **Water Activities**: Bring swimwear for a dip in the spring.
- **Bug Spray**: Essential for the hiking trails and camping areas.

4. St. George Island State Park

- **Location**: 1900 E Gulf Beach Dr, St George Island, FL 32328
- **Prices**: Campsites cost around $24 per night.
- **Side Attractions**: Pristine beaches, fishing, birdwatching, and stargazing.
- **Visitor Tips**:
- **Beach Gear**: Bring beach chairs, umbrellas, and sunscreen.
- **Fishing Licenses**: Obtain a Florida fishing license if planning to fish.
- **Night Sky**: Clear nights offer excellent stargazing; bring a telescope or binoculars.

5. Stephen Foster Folk Culture Center State Park

- **Location**: 11016 Lillian Saunders Dr, White Springs, FL 32096
- **Prices**: Campsites range from $16 to $25 per night. Cabins are available for about $100 per night.
- **Side Attractions**: Suwannee River, folk art museum, annual folk festivals.
- **Visitor Tips**:
- **Cultural Events**: Check the park's schedule for festivals and events.

- **River Activities**: Canoeing and kayaking are popular; rentals available nearby.
- **Art and Crafts**: Explore the craft square and workshops.

6. Falling Waters State Park

- **Location**: 1130 State Park Road, Chipley, FL 32428
- **Prices**: Campsites are approximately $18 per night.
- **Side Attractions**: Florida's tallest waterfall, sinkholes, nature trails.
- **Visitor Tips**:
- **Waterfall Viewing**: Best after heavy rains when the waterfall is most impressive.
- **Hiking Boots**: Necessary for navigating the trails and sinkholes.
- **Photography**: Don't forget your camera for capturing the park's unique features.

7. Grayton Beach State Park

- **Location**: 357 Main Park Rd, Santa Rosa Beach, FL 32459
- **Prices**: Campsites are about $30 per night. Cabins range from $110 to $160 per night.
- **Side Attractions**: Sugar-white sand beaches, Western Lake for kayaking and paddleboarding.
- **Visitor Tips**:
- **Beach Activities**: Bring snorkeling gear and beach games.
- **Cabin Reservations**: Book well in advance, as cabins are highly sought after.
- **Sunrise and Sunset**: Plan to watch the sunrise or sunset over the Gulf for breathtaking views.

8. Ochlockonee River State Park

- **Location**: 429 State Park Rd, Sopchoppy, FL 32358
- **Prices**: Campsites cost around $16 per night.
- **Side Attractions**: Canoeing on the Ochlockonee River, wildlife viewing, hiking trails.
- **Visitor Tips**:
- **Canoe/Kayak Rentals**: Available in the park for exploring the river.
- **Wildlife Awareness**: Be prepared to see diverse wildlife, including white squirrels and red-cockaded woodpeckers.
- **Quiet Hours**: Respect the park's quiet hours to enjoy the natural sounds of the environment.

9. Manatee Springs State Park

- **Location**: 11650 NW 115 St, Chiefland, FL 32626
- **Prices**: Campsites are about $20 per night.
- **Side Attractions**: Manatee viewing in winter, swimming and snorkeling in the spring, Suwannee River.
- **Visitor Tips**:
- **Winter Visit**: Visit in winter to see manatees in the springs.
- **Swim Gear**: Bring snorkels and swimsuits for the crystal-clear spring waters.
- **Picnic Supplies**: Picnic areas are plentiful; pack a lunch to enjoy by the water.

General Tips for Visitors

- **Reservations**: Many state parks recommend or require reservations for camping and cabins, especially during peak

seasons. Book early to secure your spot.
- **Check Weather**: Northern Florida's weather can vary; check forecasts before your trip and pack accordingly.
- **Pack Essentials**: Sunscreen, insect repellent, and plenty of water are essential for outdoor activities.
- **Leave No Trace**: Practice Leave No Trace principles to help preserve the natural beauty of these parks.
- **Wildlife Safety**: Respect wildlife by observing from a distance and never feeding animals.
- **Park Maps**: Obtain a park map at the entrance or visitor center to navigate the trails and attractions efficiently.

These accommodation options in Northern Florida offer a variety of experiences, from camping under the stars to staying in cozy cabins, all while being surrounded by the natural beauty and rich history of the region.

Local Flora and Fauna of Northern Florida

Northern Florida is home to a diverse range of ecosystems, including forests, wetlands, coastal areas, and rivers, each supporting a rich variety of plant and animal species. This region's unique climate and geography create habitats that are home to numerous native flora and fauna.

Flora

1. **Longleaf Pine (Pinus palustris)**

- **Description**: Tall, straight pine trees with long needles and large cones.
- **Habitat**: Common in sandy soils and pine flatwoods.
- **Ecological Importance**: Provides habitat for many species, including the endangered red-cockaded woodpecker.

1. **Saw Palmetto (Serenoa repens)**

- **Description**: A low-growing palm with fan-shaped leaves and sharp, saw-like edges.
- **Habitat**: Found in pine forests, scrublands, and coastal areas.
- **Uses**: Historically used by Native Americans for food and medicine; modern uses include supplements.

1. **Southern Magnolia (Magnolia grandiflora)**

- **Description**: Large, evergreen tree with glossy leaves and fragrant white flowers.
- **Habitat**: Common in hardwood forests and mixed woodlands.
- **Ecological Importance**: Provides food and shelter for wildlife; its flowers attract pollinators.

1. **Cypress Trees (Taxodium spp.)**

- **Description**: Deciduous conifers with knobby roots, known as "knees," that protrude above the water surface.
- **Habitat**: Found in swamps and along riverbanks.
- **Ecological Importance**: Important for water filtration and providing habitat for wetland species.

1. **Wiregrass (Aristida stricta)**

- **Description**: A perennial grass with fine, wiry stems.
- **Habitat**: Dominates the understory in pine flatwoods and savannas.
- **Ecological Importance**: Key component of fire-maintained ecosystems; provides habitat for gopher tortoises and other species.

Fauna

1. **American Alligator (Alligator mississippiensis)**

- **Description**: Large reptile with a broad snout, powerful tail, and armored body.
- **Habitat**: Freshwater rivers, swamps, marshes, and lakes.
- **Ecological Importance**: Apex predator; helps control populations of other animals and creates "gator holes" that provide habitats for other species during dry periods.

1. **Florida Black Bear (Ursus americanus floridanus)**

- **Description**: Large, black-furred mammal with a distinct white chest patch.
- **Habitat**: Prefers forests, swamps, and scrublands.
- **Ecological Importance**: Helps disperse seeds and maintain healthy forest ecosystems through their foraging habits.

1. **Red-cockaded Woodpecker (Picoides borealis)**

- **Description**: Small woodpecker with black and white barred

back, white cheek patches, and a small red spot on males.
- **Habitat**: Old-growth pine forests, especially longleaf pine.
- **Conservation Status**: Endangered due to habitat loss; relies on mature pine forests for nesting.

1. **Gopher Tortoise (Gopherus polyphemus)**

- **Description**: Medium-sized terrestrial turtle with a domed shell and stout, elephantine legs.
- **Habitat**: Sandy soils in pine forests, scrublands, and coastal dunes.
- **Ecological Importance**: Keystone species; their burrows provide habitats for over 350 other species.

1. **Eastern Indigo Snake (Drymarchon couperi)**

- **Description**: Large, glossy black snake with iridescent blue-black scales.
- **Habitat**: Pine forests, hardwood hammocks, and wet prairies.
- **Conservation Status**: Threatened; relies on gopher tortoise burrows for shelter.

1. **Manatee (Trichechus manatus)**

- **Description**: Large, slow-moving marine mammals with paddle-shaped flippers and a spoon-shaped tail.
- **Habitat**: Coastal waters, estuaries, and slow-moving rivers with abundant vegetation.
- **Ecological Importance**: Help maintain healthy aquatic ecosystems by grazing on seagrass and algae.

1. **Bald Eagle (Haliaeetus leucocephalus)**

- **Description**: Large bird of prey with a distinctive white head and tail, and a dark brown body.
- **Habitat**: Near large bodies of open water with abundant fish and mature trees for nesting.
- **Ecological Importance**: Apex predator; plays a crucial role in maintaining the balance of fish populations.

1. **Eastern Gray Squirrel (Sciurus carolinensis)**

- **Description**: Medium-sized tree squirrel with gray fur and a bushy tail.
- **Habitat**: Hardwood forests, suburban areas, and parks.
- **Ecological Importance**: Important seed disperser, aiding in forest regeneration.

Conservation Efforts

Northern Florida's diverse ecosystems face threats from habitat loss, pollution, and climate change. Various conservation efforts are in place to protect these unique environments and their inhabitants:

- **Protected Areas**: Establishing and maintaining state parks, national forests, and wildlife refuges to preserve natural habitats.
- **Restoration Projects**: Efforts to restore longleaf pine ecosystems and wetlands, which are crucial for many species.
- **Wildlife Corridors**: Creating corridors to connect fragmented habitats, allowing wildlife to move safely between

areas.
- **Public Education**: Programs to raise awareness about the importance of conservation and sustainable practices.

By exploring and appreciating the flora and fauna of Northern Florida, visitors can gain a deeper understanding of the region's natural beauty and the importance of preserving it for future generations.

2

Chapter 2

CENTRAL FLORIDA STATE PARKS

Central Florida is a dynamic region known for its diverse landscapes, vibrant cities, and rich cultural heritage. Stretching from the Gulf of Mexico to the Atlantic Ocean, Central Florida encompasses a variety of environments, including bustling urban centers, tranquil lakes, lush forests, and expansive wetlands. The region is perhaps best known for its world-renowned theme parks, including Walt Disney World, Universal Studios, and SeaWorld, which attract millions of visitors annually. However, beyond the theme parks, Central Florida offers a wealth of natural beauty and outdoor activities.

The area is characterized by its numerous freshwater springs, rivers, and lakes, making it a haven for water sports enthusiasts. Popular activities include kayaking, canoeing, fishing, and paddleboarding. The Wekiva River, Rainbow Springs, and Silver Springs are notable destinations where visitors can explore crystal-clear waters and observe a variety of wildlife, including manatees, alligators, and numerous bird species.

Central Florida is also rich in history and culture. The city of Orlando, the region's largest urban area, boasts a thriving arts scene, with numerous museums, galleries, and theaters. Historic towns like Winter Park and Mount Dora offer charming downtown areas with boutique shopping, fine dining, and cultural festivals. The region's agricultural heritage is celebrated through various farmers' markets and festivals, highlighting local produce such as citrus fruits, strawberries, and blueberries.

In addition to its natural and cultural attractions, Central Florida is home to several state parks and protected areas. These include the Ocala National Forest, known for its extensive trail system and diverse ecosystems, and the Merritt Island National Wildlife Refuge, which provides critical habitat for a variety of species. These protected areas offer opportunities for hiking, camping, birdwatching, and wildlife photography.

Central Florida's climate is subtropical, with hot, humid summers and mild, dry winters. This makes it an ideal destination for outdoor activities year-round. The region's tourism infrastructure is well-developed, with a wide range of accommodation options, from luxury resorts to campgrounds, catering to all types of travelers.

Overall, Central Florida is a region of contrasts and diversity, offering something for everyone. Whether you are seeking adventure in the great outdoors, cultural experiences in vibrant cities, or relaxation in serene natural settings, Central Florida provides a rich and varied landscape to explore.

Wekiwa Springs State Park

Wekiwa Springs State Park, located near Apopka, Florida, is a natural oasis known for its crystal-clear springs, lush landscapes, and abundant wildlife. The park's name "Wekiwa" is derived from the Creek Indian word meaning "spring of water," highlighting the area's historical significance to indigenous peoples who relied on the springs for water and sustenance. The park was established in 1969, preserving over 7,000 acres of Florida's diverse ecosystems, including wetlands, hammocks, and pine flatwoods. Its springs, which flow into the Wekiva River, have been a popular destination for recreation and relaxation for centuries, first for Native Americans and later for European settlers and modern-day visitors.

Location

- **Address**: 1800 Wekiwa Circle, Apopka, FL 32712
- **GPS Coordinates**: 28.7119° N, 81.4635° W
- **Directions**: The park is located about 20 miles north of Orlando. From Orlando, take I-4 west to Exit 92 for FL-436. Continue on FL-436 to Wekiwa Springs Road, then follow signs to the park entrance.

Main Attractions

- **Wekiwa Springs**: The park's centerpiece, offering cool,

clear water for swimming and snorkeling. The spring maintains a year-round temperature of 72°F.
- **Wekiva River**: A scenic river perfect for canoeing and kayaking. Visitors can explore the serene waterway and observe a variety of wildlife.
- **Sandhill Habitat**: Unique upland area home to diverse plant and animal species, providing excellent hiking opportunities.

Prices

- **Admission Fee**: $6 per vehicle (2-8 people), $4 for single-occupant vehicles, $2 for pedestrians, bicyclists, extra passengers, or passengers in vehicles with holders of Annual Individual Entrance Pass.
- **Canoe/Kayak Rentals**: Prices range from $20 to $30 for half-day rentals.

Activities

- **Swimming**: The spring-fed swimming area is approximately 20 feet deep at its deepest point and perfect for cooling off.
- **Canoeing/Kayaking**: The Wekiva River and Rock Springs Run provide paddling opportunities through scenic landscapes.
- **Hiking**: Over 13 miles of trails range from easy to moderate, allowing visitors to explore different habitats.
- **Biking**: Designated biking trails for mountain biking enthusiasts.
- **Wildlife Viewing**: Common sightings include deer, black

bears, turkeys, and a variety of bird species.

Facilities

- **Picnic Areas**: Multiple picnic pavilions and tables with grills are available for use.
- **Campgrounds**: Tent and RV campsites with water and electrical hookups, as well as primitive campsites for a more rustic experience.
- **Restrooms and Showers**: Modern facilities located throughout the park.
- **Concession Stand**: Offers snacks, drinks, and rental equipment for various activities.
- **Visitor Center**: Provides information about the park's history, wildlife, and conservation efforts.

Trails and Activities

- **Main Hiking Trails**:
- **Orange Trail**: A 5.3-mile loop trail offering scenic views of the park's sandhill habitat.
- **White Trail**: A shorter, 1.8-mile loop ideal for a quick hike through the diverse landscape.
- **Blue Trail**: A 2.7-mile trail leading to the Wekiva River, perfect for observing wildlife.
- **Biking Trails**: Designated areas for off-road biking enthusiasts.
- **Equestrian Trails**: Available for horseback riding, with designated parking for horse trailers.

Visitor Tips

- **Early Arrival**: The park can reach capacity, especially on weekends and holidays. Arrive early to ensure entry.
- **Swimming Safety**: The spring area has a roped-off section for swimming; always supervise children and non-swimmers.
- **Stay Hydrated**: Bring plenty of water, especially during the hot summer months.
- **Sun Protection**: Wear sunscreen, hats, and sunglasses to protect against the strong Florida sun.
- **Wildlife Caution**: Keep a safe distance from all wildlife, do not feed animals, and secure food to avoid attracting bears.
- **Trail Preparedness**: Wear sturdy shoes, bring insect repellent, and carry a map or GPS device.
- **Leave No Trace**: Follow Leave No Trace principles to help keep the park pristine. Pack out all trash and be mindful of the environment.

Wekiwa Springs State Park offers a perfect blend of natural beauty and recreational opportunities, making it a must-visit destination for anyone exploring Central Florida. Whether you're looking to swim in the refreshing springs, paddle down a scenic river, or hike through diverse landscapes, the park provides a serene escape from the hustle and bustle of everyday life.

Blue Spring State Park

Blue Spring State Park, located in Orange City, Florida, is a renowned natural haven famous for its crystal-clear spring waters and winter manatee gatherings. The park encompasses over 2,600 acres, including the largest spring on the St. Johns River, Blue Spring, which has a year-round temperature of 72°F. The spring and surrounding areas have a rich history, once home to Native American tribes and later settled by European explorers. The park was established in 1972 to protect the spring and its ecosystem, particularly the West Indian manatees that seek refuge in the warm waters during the colder months. Blue Spring has since become a focal point for conservation efforts and a popular destination for nature enthusiasts.

Location

- **Address**: 2100 W French Avenue, Orange City, FL 32763
- **GPS Coordinates**: 28.9479° N, 81.3396° W
- **Directions**: From I-4, take Exit 114 and head west on FL-472. Turn right onto US-17 N/US-92 E, then left onto W French Avenue. Follow signs to the park entrance.

Main Attractions

- **Blue Spring**: The park's main feature, offering opportunities for swimming, snorkeling, and manatee viewing. The spring's depth is around 120 feet at its deepest point.
- **Manatee Observation**: From mid-November to March, the park becomes a sanctuary for hundreds of manatees seeking warm waters.

- **St. Johns River**: Provides additional recreational activities like boating, fishing, and wildlife observation.

Prices

- **Admission Fee**: $6 per vehicle (2-8 people), $4 for single-occupant vehicles, $2 for pedestrians, bicyclists, extra passengers, or passengers in vehicles with holders of Annual Individual Entrance Pass.
- **Boat Tours**: Eco-tours on the St. Johns River are available for around $25 per adult and $15 per child.
- **Kayak/Canoe Rentals**: Prices range from $20 to $30 for half-day rentals.

Activities

- **Swimming and Snorkeling**: The spring's clear, cool waters are ideal for these activities, with a designated swimming area.
- **Scuba Diving**: Allowed in the spring with appropriate certification; depth reaches up to 120 feet.
- **Hiking**: Several trails, including a 4.5-mile Pine Island Trail, offer scenic views of the park's diverse ecosystems.
- **Wildlife Viewing**: Excellent opportunities to see manatees, alligators, and various bird species.
- **Boating and Fishing**: Permitted on the St. Johns River, with boat ramps available in the park.

Facilities

- **Picnic Areas**: Numerous picnic tables and pavilions

equipped with grills.
- **Campgrounds**: 51 campsites with water and electrical hookups, as well as primitive campsites for a more rustic experience.
- **Restrooms and Showers**: Modern facilities located throughout the park.
- **Concession Stand**: Offers snacks, drinks, and rental equipment.
- **Visitor Center**: Provides educational exhibits about the park's history, wildlife, and conservation efforts.

Trails and Activities

- **Pine Island Trail**: A 4.5-mile trail through the park's wetlands and hammocks, ideal for hiking and wildlife observation.
- **Blue Spring Run**: A short trail leading to the spring, perfect for a leisurely walk and manatee viewing.
- **River Tours**: Guided eco-tours along the St. Johns River, showcasing the region's flora and fauna.

Visitor Tips

- **Early Arrival**: The park can reach capacity, especially during manatee season and weekends. Arrive early to ensure entry.
- **Swimming Restrictions**: Swimming is not allowed when manatees are present (mid-November to March) to protect the animals.
- **Stay Hydrated**: Bring plenty of water, especially during the hot summer months.
- **Sun Protection**: Wear sunscreen, hats, and sunglasses to

protect against the strong Florida sun.
- **Wildlife Caution**: Keep a safe distance from all wildlife, do not feed animals, and secure food to avoid attracting raccoons and other wildlife.
- **Trail Preparedness**: Wear sturdy shoes, bring insect repellent, and carry a map or GPS device.
- **Leave No Trace**: Follow Leave No Trace principles to help keep the park pristine. Pack out all trash and be mindful of the environment.
- **Manatee Etiquette**: Observe manatees from a distance and avoid disturbing them. Use viewing platforms for the best experience.

Blue Spring State Park offers a unique combination of natural beauty and recreational opportunities, making it a must-visit destination in Central Florida. Whether you're exploring the refreshing spring, paddling down the St. Johns River, or observing the gentle manatees, the park provides a serene and captivating experience for all visitors.

De Leon Springs State Park

De Leon Springs State Park, located in Volusia County, Florida, is a scenic natural area known for its historic significance and outdoor recreational opportunities. The park's name originates from Spanish explorer Juan Ponce de León, who is said to have visited the area in search of the Fountain of Youth. The spring within the park has been a gathering place for thousands of years, first by Native American tribes and later by settlers who established sugar plantations around its shores. The park was established in 1982 to protect the natural beauty of the spring and surrounding habitats, offering visitors a glimpse into Florida's ecological and historical heritage.

Location

- **Address**: 601 Ponce de Leon Blvd, De Leon Springs, FL 32130
- **GPS Coordinates**: 29.1344° N, 81.3577° W
- **Directions**: From I-4, take Exit 114 and head north on FL-472. Continue on FL-472 until you reach Ponce de Leon Blvd. Follow signs to the park entrance.

Main Attractions

- **Spring Swimming**: The main attraction is the spring itself, where visitors can swim, snorkel, and enjoy the cool, clear waters year-round.
- **Paddleboat and Kayak Rentals**: Available for exploring the spring run and nearby Lake Woodruff National Wildlife Refuge.
- **Old Spanish Sugar Mill Restaurant**: A historic restaurant where visitors can cook their own pancakes at their table, utilizing griddles built into each table.
- **Historic Site**: Explore the remains of the 1830s sugar mill and learn about the area's agricultural history.

Prices

- **Admission Fee**: $6 per vehicle (2-8 people), $4 for single-occupant vehicles, $2 for pedestrians, bicyclists, extra

passengers, or passengers in vehicles with holders of Annual Individual Entrance Pass.
- **Paddleboat and Kayak Rentals**: Prices range from $15 to $20 per hour.

Activities

- **Swimming**: The spring maintains a constant temperature of 72°F and is perfect for cooling off on hot days.
- **Boating**: Rent paddleboats or kayaks to explore the spring run and Lake Woodruff National Wildlife Refuge.
- **Wildlife Viewing**: Excellent birdwatching opportunities throughout the park, especially along the spring run and in the nearby wildlife refuge.
- **Picnicking**: Numerous picnic areas with tables and grills available for day-use visitors.

Facilities

- **Restaurant**: The Old Spanish Sugar Mill Restaurant offers unique dining experiences and is a popular spot for breakfast and lunch.
- **Picnic Areas**: Shaded picnic pavilions and tables with grills throughout the park.
- **Restrooms and Changing Facilities**: Modern facilities located near the swimming area.
- **Gift Shop**: Offers souvenirs, snacks, and basic supplies.
- **Visitor Center**: Provides information about the park's history, wildlife, and recreational activities.

Trails and Activities

- **Spring Run Trail**: A short trail leading along the spring run, offering scenic views of the crystal-clear water.
- **Lake Woodruff National Wildlife Refuge**: Accessible via kayak or paddleboat, with opportunities for wildlife observation and photography.

Visitor Tips

- **Restaurant Reservations**: If planning to visit the Old Spanish Sugar Mill Restaurant, make reservations in advance, especially on weekends.
- **Swimming Safety**: Always swim in designated areas and supervise children closely.
- **Wildlife Awareness**: Respect wildlife and observe from a safe distance; do not feed or approach animals.
- **Sun Protection**: Wear sunscreen, hats, and sunglasses to protect against the sun, especially during peak hours.
- **Water Activities**: Bring appropriate attire for swimming or boating, and consider renting equipment for a more enjoyable experience.

De Leon Springs State Park offers a blend of natural beauty, historical intrigue, and recreational opportunities, making it a perfect destination for visitors seeking to explore Florida's diverse landscapes and cultural heritage.

Lake Louisa State Park

Lake Louisa State Park, located in Clermont, Florida, is a beautiful and expansive park known for its picturesque landscapes, tranquil lakes, and diverse wildlife. Established in 1970, the park covers over 4,000 acres and is named after the serene Lake Louisa, one of the park's main attractions. The area was originally part of a large citrus plantation and has since been transformed into a state park, preserving its natural beauty and offering visitors a variety of recreational opportunities. The park's rich history includes its role in Florida's agricultural heritage, particularly in the citrus industry, and its transformation into a sanctuary for outdoor enthusiasts and nature lovers.

Location

- **Address**: 7305 US-27, Clermont, FL 34714
- **GPS Coordinates**: 28.4874° N, 81.7660° W
- **Directions**: From Orlando, take Florida's Turnpike to Exit 285, then head west on US-27 for about 5 miles. The park entrance will be on the right.

Main Attractions

- **Lake Louisa**: The centerpiece of the park, offering stunning views, swimming, boating, and fishing. The lake is approximately 180 acres and has a maximum depth of 40 feet.
- **Hiking Trails**: The park features over 20 miles of trails, ranging from easy walks to challenging hikes, through diverse habitats.

- **Equestrian Trails**: A network of trails designed for horseback riding, allowing riders to explore the park's scenic landscapes.
- **Historic Citrus Packing House**: A restored packing house from the area's citrus farming days, offering a glimpse into Florida's agricultural past.

Prices

- **Admission Fee**: $5 per vehicle (2-8 people), $4 for single-occupant vehicles, $2 for pedestrians, bicyclists, extra passengers, or passengers in vehicles with holders of Annual Individual Entrance Pass.
- **Canoe/Kayak Rentals**: Available for $10 per hour or $30 for a half-day rental.

Activities

- **Swimming**: Designated swimming area on Lake Louisa's sandy beach, with clear, refreshing waters perfect for a swim.
- **Boating and Fishing**: Canoes, kayaks, and small boats are welcome on the lake. Fishing is popular, with species including bass, bluegill, and catfish.
- **Hiking**: Over 20 miles of trails, including the Lake Louisa Trail and the Palmetto Trail, offer opportunities for birdwatching and nature photography.
- **Horseback Riding**: Equestrian trails are available, providing scenic routes through pine forests and along lake shores.
- **Camping**: The park offers campsites with water and electric hookups, as well as primitive campsites for a more rustic

experience.

Facilities

- **Campgrounds**: Equipped with 60 campsites, including 20 with water and electric hookups, and 40 primitive sites.
- **Picnic Areas**: Numerous picnic pavilions and tables with grills available throughout the park.
- **Restrooms and Showers**: Clean, accessible facilities located near the camping and picnic areas.
- **Visitor Center**: Offers educational exhibits about the park's wildlife, history, and conservation efforts.

Trails and Activities

- **Lake Louisa Trail**: A 5.5-mile loop trail that circles Lake Louisa, providing stunning views and opportunities for wildlife observation.
- **Palmetto Trail**: A 3.6-mile trail that traverses through diverse habitats, featuring scenic vistas and shaded paths.
- **Equestrian Trails**: Over 6 miles of trails designed for horseback riding, including the Orange Trail and the Lake Trail.

Visitor Tips

- **Swimming Safety**: Always swim in designated areas and be aware of weather conditions. Lifeguards are not on duty.
- **Wildlife Caution**: Keep a safe distance from all wildlife, including alligators, and do not feed animals.
- **Trail Etiquette**: Stay on designated trails, wear sturdy shoes,

and bring plenty of water. Keep pets on a leash and clean up after them.
- **Reservations**: For camping or group use, make reservations well in advance, especially during peak seasons.
- **Sun Protection**: Wear sunscreen, hats, and sunglasses, and bring insect repellent to protect against mosquitoes.
- **Stay Hydrated**: Bring plenty of water, especially during the hotter months, and be mindful of the sun's intensity.

Lake Louisa State Park offers a perfect blend of natural beauty, recreational activities, and historical interest, making it an ideal destination for families, hikers, anglers, and nature enthusiasts. Whether you are looking to relax by the lake, explore scenic trails, or immerse yourself in the park's rich history, Lake Louisa State Park provides a serene escape into Florida's natural wilderness.

Outdoor Activities and Adventures

Central Florida offers a wealth of outdoor activities and adventures, catering to nature lovers, adventure seekers, and those looking to explore the region's diverse landscapes. Here's a detailed look at some of the top outdoor activities you can enjoy in Central Florida:

1. Water Sports and Springs Exploration

Central Florida is renowned for its crystal-clear springs and water bodies, offering various water sports and activities:

- **Canoeing and Kayaking**: Explore scenic waterways like the Wekiva River, Rainbow River, and Silver River. These rivers are ideal for paddling, with opportunities to spot wildlife such as manatees, alligators, and numerous bird species.
- **Swimming and Snorkeling**: Visit springs like Wekiwa Springs, Blue Spring, and Rock Springs for refreshing swims in clear, cool waters. These springs also offer snorkeling opportunities to observe underwater life.
- **Tubing**: Enjoy tubing down spring-fed rivers like the Ichetucknee River, a relaxing way to experience the natural beauty of Florida.

2. Hiking and Nature Trails

Central Florida boasts numerous trails that wind through diverse landscapes, from pine forests to wetlands and lakeshores:

- **State Parks**: Explore trails in popular state parks like Lake Louisa State Park, with its Lake Louisa Trail offering scenic lake views. The Ocala National Forest provides extensive trail systems, including the Florida Trail for longer hikes.
- **Wildlife Viewing**: Many trails offer excellent opportunities for birdwatching and wildlife observation. Keep an eye out for Florida's native species, including deer, tortoises, and a variety of bird species.

3. Biking and Mountain Biking

- **Scenic Routes**: Enjoy cycling along dedicated bike trails in parks like Santos Trailhead & Campground in Ocala, offering challenging terrain and scenic views.
- **Mountain Biking**: Santos Trailhead features over 80 miles

of singletrack trails, attracting mountain biking enthusiasts from around the country.

4. Camping and Outdoor Recreation

- **Campgrounds**: Central Florida's state parks and national forests offer campsites for both tent camping and RVs. Enjoy amenities like campfire cooking, stargazing, and connecting with nature.
- **Fishing**: Central Florida's lakes and rivers provide excellent fishing opportunities, with species including bass, crappie, and catfish. Many parks offer boat ramps and fishing piers for anglers.

5. Eco-Tours and Wildlife Encounters

- **Airboat Tours**: Take an airboat tour through the Everglades or Lake Tohopekaliga for an exhilarating ride and the chance to see alligators and other wildlife up close.
- **Wildlife Sanctuaries**: Visit wildlife sanctuaries and refuges like the Merritt Island National Wildlife Refuge, home to diverse ecosystems and species such as manatees, dolphins, and migratory birds.

6. Rock Climbing and Adventure Parks

- **Indoor Climbing**: Explore indoor rock climbing gyms in urban areas like Orlando for a challenging workout and skill-building experience.
- **Adventure Parks**: Visit adventure parks offering ziplining, rope courses, and other outdoor challenges, such as Tree

Trek Adventure Park.

7. Hot Air Ballooning and Skydiving

- **Hot Air Ballooning**: Experience Central Florida's scenic beauty from above with hot air balloon rides, offering panoramic views of lakes, forests, and even theme parks.
- **Skydiving**: For thrill-seekers, tandem skydiving experiences are available in the region, providing an adrenaline rush and breathtaking aerial views.

8. Golfing and Outdoor Sports

- **Golf Courses**: Central Florida is known for its championship golf courses, offering challenging layouts and scenic views. Enjoy golfing amidst lush landscapes and serene lakes.
- **Outdoor Sports**: Engage in various outdoor sports such as tennis, volleyball, and basketball at parks and resorts throughout the region.

9. Photography and Nature Walks

- **Photography**: Central Florida's natural beauty provides ample opportunities for photography enthusiasts. Capture stunning landscapes, wildlife, and unique ecosystems.
- **Nature Walks**: Join guided nature walks led by park rangers or naturalists, offering educational insights into the region's flora, fauna, and conservation efforts.

10. Cultural and Historical Tours

- **Historic Sites**: Explore historic sites and museums that showcase Central Florida's rich cultural heritage, including pioneer settlements, Native American history, and citrus farming.

Central Florida's outdoor activities cater to a wide range of interests and skill levels, ensuring there's something for everyone to enjoy in this diverse and vibrant region. Whether you prefer adrenaline-pumping adventures, serene nature walks, or cultural explorations, Central Florida offers endless opportunities to connect with the outdoors and create unforgettable experiences.

Accommodation Options In Central Florida

Here's a detailed overview of accommodation options in Central Florida, including addresses, prices, side attractions, and visitor requirements where applicable:

1. Hotels and Resorts
a. **Walt Disney World Resorts**

- **Address**: Various locations within Walt Disney World Resort, Lake Buena Vista, FL 32830
- **Prices**: Varied depending on the resort and season. Typically ranges from $150 to over $500 per night.
- **Side Attractions**: Access to Disney theme parks, water parks, golf courses, and entertainment areas.
- **Visitor Requirements**: Resort guests may have access to

early park entry and other benefits. Check specific resort policies for details.

b. Universal Orlando Resort Hotels

- **Address**: Various locations within Universal Orlando Resort, Orlando, FL 32819
- **Prices**: Rates vary by hotel and season, typically starting from $150 per night.
- **Side Attractions**: Proximity to Universal Studios Florida, Islands of Adventure, Volcano Bay, CityWalk entertainment complex.
- **Visitor Requirements**: Guests may enjoy early park admission to Universal theme parks. Benefits vary by hotel tier.

c. Marriott World Center Orlando

- **Address**: 8701 World Center Drive, Orlando, FL 32821
- **Prices**: Rates vary; typically around $200 to $400 per night.
- **Side Attractions**: Golf course, multiple pools, restaurants, spa, and proximity to Walt Disney World and other attractions.
- **Visitor Requirements**: Check-in requirements include a valid ID and credit card for incidentals.

2. Vacation Rentals and Villas
a. Vacation Home Rentals

- **Address**: Various locations throughout Central Florida (e.g., Kissimmee, Davenport)
- **Prices**: Varies widely based on size, amenities, and location.

Typically $100 to $300+ per night.
- **Side Attractions**: Private pools, game rooms, themed rooms, and proximity to theme parks and shopping areas.
- **Visitor Requirements**: Booking typically requires a deposit, and specific property rules may apply regarding occupancy and amenities.

b. **Airbnb and VRBO Listings**

- **Address**: Various locations across Central Florida
- **Prices**: Varies widely based on property type, location, and amenities. Typically $50 to $300+ per night.
- **Side Attractions**: Unique accommodations, local experiences, and proximity to attractions.
- **Visitor Requirements**: Guests must adhere to host rules, check-in procedures, and may require a security deposit.

3. **Campgrounds and RV Parks**
   a. **Disney's Fort Wilderness Resort & Campground**

- **Address**: 4510 Fort Wilderness Trail, Orlando, FL 32830
- **Prices**: Tent and RV sites start around $80 to $160 per night; cabins range from $350 to $600+ per night.
- **Side Attractions**: Wilderness activities, outdoor movies, boat rentals, and easy access to Disney parks.
- **Visitor Requirements**: Campers must adhere to Disney's camping policies, including check-in procedures and campground rules.

b. **KOA Campgrounds**

- **Address**: Multiple locations in Central Florida (e.g., Kissimmee, Clermont)
- **Prices**: Tent sites start around $50 to $70 per night; RV sites range from $60 to $100+ per night.
- **Side Attractions**: Pool, playground, mini-golf, and close proximity to attractions like Disney and Universal.
- **Visitor Requirements**: Reservations typically required, and guests must follow campground rules regarding pets, noise, and campfires.

Visitor Tips

- **Booking in Advance**: Especially during peak seasons and holidays, it's advisable to book accommodations well in advance.
- **Theme Park Benefits**: Staying at on-site resorts often includes perks like early park admission and transportation options.
- **Check Policies**: Each accommodation type may have specific cancellation policies, check-in times, and amenity details that visitors should review before booking.

These options provide a range of choices to suit different preferences and budgets, ensuring visitors can enjoy their stay while exploring the attractions and natural beauty of Central Florida.

Local Flora and Fauna

Central Florida's diverse ecosystems support a rich variety of flora and fauna, showcasing a unique blend of subtropical and temperate species. Here's a detailed look at the local flora and fauna found in Central Florida:

Flora

1. **Longleaf Pine Forests**:

- **Description**: Once widespread in the region, these forests are characterized by towering longleaf pines, wiregrass understory, and a diverse array of wildflowers.
- **Locations**: Found in protected areas like Ocala National Forest and Tiger Bay State Forest.

1. **Wetlands and Marshes**:

- **Description**: Central Florida's wetlands, including marshes and swamps, are vital habitats for numerous plant species adapted to waterlogged conditions.
- **Locations**: Places like Lake Kissimmee State Park and Tosohatchee Wildlife Management Area feature extensive wetland habitats.

1. **Cypress Swamps**:

- **Description**: Cypress swamps are dominated by bald cypress trees with characteristic knees protruding from the water, providing habitat for aquatic plants and animals.

- **Locations**: Big Cypress National Preserve and Econlockhatchee River feature notable cypress swamp ecosystems.

1. **Scrub and Sandhill Habitats**:

- **Description**: Scrub habitats are characterized by sandy soils and drought-resistant plants, while sandhill habitats feature rolling sandy terrain with scattered pine trees.
- **Locations**: Examples include the Lake Wales Ridge and scrub areas within Jonathan Dickinson State Park.

1. **Native Wildflowers**:

- **Description**: Central Florida's native wildflowers include species like Coreopsis (Florida's state wildflower), Blanketflower, and Butterfly Milkweed, attracting pollinators like butterflies and bees.
- **Locations**: Found along roadsides, in state parks, and natural areas throughout the region.

Fauna

1. **American Alligator**:

- **Description**: Common throughout Central Florida, alligators inhabit freshwater lakes, rivers, and marshes, playing a crucial role in local ecosystems.
- **Locations**: Seen in places like Lake Tohopekaliga, Lake Kissimmee, and the Everglades.

1. **Florida Panther**:

- **Description**: A critically endangered species, the Florida panther is a large carnivore native to Florida, primarily found in remote and protected areas.
- **Locations**: Occurs in scattered locations such as the Florida Panther National Wildlife Refuge and Big Cypress National Preserve.

1. **Manatees**:

- **Description**: Often seen in Central Florida's freshwater springs and rivers, manatees are gentle herbivores that seek warm water refuges during cooler months.
- **Locations**: Blue Spring State Park, Crystal River National Wildlife Refuge, and other spring-fed rivers.

1. **Bird Species**:

- **Description**: Central Florida is a haven for birdwatchers, with over 500 bird species recorded. Species include Bald Eagles, Sandhill Cranes, and numerous migratory birds.
- **Locations**: Merritt Island National Wildlife Refuge, Paynes Prairie Preserve State Park, and numerous state parks and natural areas.

1. **Gopher Tortoise**:

- **Description**: A keystone species in Florida's ecosystems, gopher tortoises create burrows that provide shelter for over 350 other species, including snakes and small mammals.
- **Locations**: Found in sandy habitats like scrub areas, sandhills, and pine forests.

Conservation Efforts

- **Land Preservation**: Organizations and government agencies work to protect and restore natural habitats through land acquisition and management practices.
- **Species Recovery Programs**: Initiatives like the Florida Panther Recovery Program aim to increase population numbers and ensure the survival of endangered species.
- **Restoration Projects**: Efforts to restore wetlands, improve water quality, and manage invasive species help maintain biodiversity and ecosystem health.

Central Florida's diverse flora and fauna offer a glimpse into the region's natural beauty and ecological importance. Whether exploring wetlands teeming with wildlife, hiking through pine forests, or marveling at the resilience of native plants, visitors can immerse themselves in Florida's rich natural heritage.

3

Chapter 3

SOUTHERN FLORIDA

Southern Florida is a region renowned for its vibrant culture, diverse ecosystems, and world-class attractions. Stretching from the iconic city of Miami to the tranquil Everglades National Park, Southern Florida captivates visitors with its blend of urban sophistication and natural beauty.

At the heart of Southern Florida lies Miami, a dynamic metropolis known for its stunning beaches, Art Deco architecture in South Beach, and vibrant nightlife in areas like Wynwood and Little Havana. The city's cultural mosaic reflects a rich blend of Latin American, Caribbean, and international influences, evident in its cuisine, music, and festivals.

Beyond Miami, Southern Florida offers a gateway to the unique ecosystem of the Everglades, a UNESCO World Heritage Site and International Biosphere Reserve. This expansive wetland is home to a diverse array of wildlife, including alligators, manatees, and rare bird species like the roseate spoonbill. Visitors can explore the Everglades through airboat tours, hiking trails, and wildlife observation platforms, gaining insight into its crucial role in preserving Florida's ecological balance.

Southern Florida's coastal regions boast pristine beaches such as Key Biscayne and the Florida Keys, renowned for their crystal-clear waters and coral reefs teeming with marine life. Adventure seekers can indulge in snorkeling, diving, and fishing expeditions, while history enthusiasts can explore historic sites like the Ernest Hemingway Home and Museum in Key West.

Whether seeking urban excitement, natural wonders, or cultural experiences, Southern Florida beckons with its diverse attractions and year-round sunshine, promising an unforgettable journey into the heart of the Sunshine State.

John Pennekamp Coral Reef State Park

John Pennekamp Coral Reef State Park, established in 1963, is located in Key Largo, Florida. It was the first underwater park in the United States and remains a premier destination for snorkeling, diving, and exploring the vibrant coral reefs of the Florida Keys. Named after John D. Pennekamp, a Miami newspaper editor and conservationist, the park spans approximately 70 nautical square miles and encompasses both underwater wonders and terrestrial habitats.

Location

- **Address**: 102601 Overseas Hwy, Key Largo, FL 33037
- **GPS Coordinates**: 25.1235° N, 80.4158° W
- **Directions**: Located on US-1 (Overseas Highway) in Key Largo, approximately 55 miles south of Miami. The park entrance is well-marked along the highway.

Main Attractions

- **Coral Reefs**: The park is renowned for its spectacular coral reefs, which are part of the Florida Keys National Marine Sanctuary. These reefs are home to diverse marine life, including colorful fish, sea turtles, and various coral species.
- **Christ of the Abyss**: An iconic underwater statue of Christ located within the park's boundaries, attracting snorkelers and divers alike.
- **Glass Bottom Boat Tours**: Visitors can enjoy guided tours aboard glass-bottom boats, offering panoramic views of the coral reefs and marine life without getting wet.

Prices

- **Admission Fee**: $4.50 per person for a single occupant vehicle, $2.50 for pedestrians, bicyclists, and extra passengers. Additional fees apply for boat tours and rentals.

Activities

- **Snorkeling and Diving**: Explore the underwater wonders of the coral reefs, accessible from designated snorkeling and

diving areas within the park.
- **Boating and Kayaking**: Boat rentals are available for exploring the park's coastal waters, mangrove islands, and marine sanctuary areas.
- **Fishing**: Anglers can fish in designated areas, adhering to state fishing regulations and park guidelines.

Facilities

- **Visitor Center**: Provides educational exhibits on marine life, conservation efforts, and the history of the park.
- **Picnic Areas**: Shaded picnic pavilions equipped with grills, offering scenic views of the park's natural surroundings.
- **Restrooms and Showers**: Clean facilities located near the beach and snorkeling areas for visitor convenience.

Trails and Activities

- **Nature Trails**: Short walking trails lead through coastal hammocks and mangrove forests, showcasing native flora and fauna.
- **Educational Programs**: Park rangers offer guided tours, snorkeling lessons, and educational programs focused on marine ecology and conservation.

Visitor Tips

- **Reservations**: During peak seasons and holidays, consider making reservations for boat tours and camping sites in advance.
- **Snorkeling Gear**: Bring your own snorkeling gear or rent

equipment from nearby outfitters for a comfortable underwater experience.
- **Conservation**: Respect marine life and coral reefs by adhering to park rules, such as not touching or disturbing the coral and wildlife.

John Pennekamp Coral Reef State Park offers an immersive experience into the underwater wonders of the Florida Keys, blending conservation with recreation for visitors eager to explore one of the nation's most precious marine environments.

Everglades National Park

Everglades National Park, established in 1947, is located in southern Florida and is the largest tropical wilderness in the United States. This UNESCO World Heritage Site and International Biosphere Reserve protects an unparalleled landscape of wetlands, mangroves, and sawgrass marshes. Spanning over 1.5 million acres, the park is vital for its biodiversity and ecosystem services, including flood control, water purification, and habitat for numerous endangered species.

Location

- **Address**: 40001 State Road 9336, Homestead, FL 33034
- **GPS Coordinates**: 25.2866° N, 80.8987° W
- **Directions**: Located southwest of Miami, accessible via US Highway 1 and Florida State Road 9336. Multiple entrances provide access to different regions of the park.

Main Attractions

- **Wildlife Viewing**: Encounter iconic species such as American alligators, manatees, Florida panthers, and a variety of bird species including the roseate spoonbill and bald eagle.
- **Airboat Tours**: Explore the park's freshwater marshes and mangrove swamps aboard guided airboat tours, offering close encounters with wildlife.
- **Anhinga Trail**: A popular spot for wildlife viewing and birdwatching, with opportunities to see alligators, turtles, and abundant birdlife up close.

Prices

- **Entrance Fee**: $30 per vehicle (valid for 7 days), $25 per motorcycle, $15 per pedestrian or cyclist. Annual passes are available for $55.

Activities

- **Boating**: Navigate through the park's waterways via kayak, canoe, or motorboat, exploring mangrove forests and freshwater marshes.
- **Hiking**: Over 80 miles of hiking trails wind through various habitats, from short nature walks to longer treks like the 15-mile Shark Valley Loop Trail.
- **Ranger-Led Programs**: Join educational programs and guided tours led by park rangers, focusing on ecology, wildlife conservation, and park history.

Facilities

- **Visitor Centers**: Multiple visitor centers provide information on park resources, exhibits on local wildlife, and orientation for visitors.
- **Campgrounds**: Several campgrounds offer facilities for tent camping and RVs, including Flamingo Campground and Long Pine Key Campground.
- **Restaurants and Concessions**: Dining options are available at Flamingo and the Gulf Coast Visitor Center, offering snacks, meals, and supplies.

Trails and Activities

- **Shark Valley Tram Tour**: A narrated tram tour offering insights into the park's unique ecosystem, including views from a 65-foot observation tower.
- **Backcountry Camping**: Obtain permits for primitive camping in designated areas, providing a deeper immersion into the park's wilderness.

Visitor Tips

- **Mosquito Protection**: Bring insect repellent and wear long sleeves and pants to protect against mosquitoes, especially during the wet season.
- **Weather Awareness**: Be prepared for sudden weather changes, including afternoon thunderstorms, by carrying rain gear and staying informed.
- **Wildlife Caution**: Observe wildlife from a safe distance and never feed or approach animals, respecting their natural behaviors and habitats.

Everglades National Park offers an unparalleled opportunity to explore one of America's most unique and fragile ecosystems, providing an unforgettable adventure into the heart of Florida's wilderness.

Oleta River State Park

Oleta River State Park, located in North Miami, Florida, is the largest urban park in the Florida State Park system. Established in 1980, the park covers over 1,000 acres and is renowned for its scenic mangrove forests, diverse recreational opportunities, and access to the Oleta River. Historically, the area has been significant for its natural resources and as a site for various Native American tribes, including the Tequesta and Seminole. Today, it serves as a green oasis amidst the urban sprawl of Miami-Dade County, offering residents and visitors a tranquil escape into nature.

Location

- **Address**: 3400 NE 163rd Street, North Miami Beach, FL 33160
- **GPS Coordinates**: 25.9272° N, 80.1484° W
- **Directions**: Easily accessible from I-95 and located off the 163rd Street causeway in North Miami Beach.

Main Attractions

- **Kayaking and Canoeing**: Paddle through the calm waters

of the Oleta River and explore its winding mangrove trails.
- **Mountain Biking**: The park features over 15 miles of challenging off-road biking trails suitable for all skill levels.
- **Beachfront**: A sandy beach area along Biscayne Bay offers swimming, sunbathing, and picnicking opportunities.

Prices

- **Entrance Fee**: $6 per vehicle (2-8 people), $4 for single-occupant vehicles, and $2 for pedestrians, bicyclists, and extra passengers.
- **Kayak/Canoe Rentals**: Typically range from $20 to $50 for various durations, depending on the rental provider within the park.
- **Mountain Bike Rentals**: Available at the park for around $30 for a half-day rental and $50 for a full day.

Activities

- **Water Sports**: Kayaking, canoeing, paddleboarding, and jet skiing are popular activities on the river and bay.
- **Fishing**: Anglers can fish from designated areas along the shore or from kayaks/canoes in the river.
- **Hiking and Biking**: The park offers multiple trails for hiking and biking, providing scenic views and varying levels of difficulty.

Facilities

- **Visitor Center**: Provides information, maps, and exhibits about the park's natural and cultural history.

- **Picnic Areas**: Shaded picnic pavilions with grills are available throughout the park for family gatherings and group events.
- **Restrooms and Showers**: Clean facilities are conveniently located near the beach and main activity areas.

Trails and Activities

- **Mountain Biking Trails**: Over 15 miles of trails range from beginner to advanced, winding through the park's natural landscapes.
- **Hiking Trails**: Several trails offer a closer look at the park's diverse ecosystems, including mangrove forests and coastal hammocks.
- **Guided Tours**: Park rangers and local outfitters occasionally offer guided tours, providing educational insights into the park's wildlife and habitats.

Visitor Tips

- **Plan Ahead**: Weekends and holidays can be busy, so consider visiting early in the day or during weekdays to avoid crowds.
- **Stay Hydrated**: Bring plenty of water, especially during the hot summer months, as outdoor activities can be strenuous.
- **Safety Gear**: For mountain biking, wear appropriate safety gear, including helmets and pads. When kayaking or canoeing, always wear a life jacket.
- **Wildlife Respect**: Respect the local wildlife by observing from a distance and not feeding animals. The park is home to various species, including birds, fish, and small mammals.

Oleta River State Park provides a diverse range of activities and natural beauty, making it a perfect destination for outdoor enthusiasts and families seeking a peaceful retreat within the bustling Miami metropolitan area.

Bahia Honda State Park

Bahia Honda State Park is a tropical paradise located in the Florida Keys, renowned for its stunning beaches, crystal-clear waters, and vibrant marine life. Established in 1961, the park covers approximately 524 acres and includes the iconic Bahia Honda Bridge. The name "Bahia Honda" means "deep bay" in Spanish, reflecting the park's geographical features. The park's history is closely tied to Henry Flagler's Overseas Railroad, which transformed the Florida Keys' development in the early 20th century. Today, Bahia Honda State Park is celebrated for its natural beauty and recreational opportunities, attracting visitors from around the world.

Location

- **Address**: 36850 Overseas Highway, Big Pine Key, FL 33043
- **GPS Coordinates**: 24.6614° N, 81.2754° W
- **Directions**: Located at Mile Marker 37 on U.S. Highway 1 in the lower Florida Keys, about 12 miles south of Marathon and 37 miles north of Key West.

Main Attractions

- **Beaches**: Bahia Honda features some of the most beautiful beaches in the Florida Keys, including Calusa Beach, Sandspur Beach, and Loggerhead Beach. These sandy shores are perfect for swimming, sunbathing, and snorkeling.
- **Bahia Honda Bridge**: The historic bridge offers stunning views of the surrounding waters and is a popular spot for photography and sightseeing.
- **Snorkeling and Diving**: The park's clear waters and coral reefs provide excellent conditions for snorkeling and diving, with opportunities to see tropical fish, rays, and other marine life.

Prices

- **Entrance Fee**: $8 per vehicle (2-8 people), $4 for single-occupant vehicles, and $2.50 for pedestrians, bicyclists, and extra passengers.
- **Snorkel Boat Tours**: Available for around $29 to $40 per person, including gear rental.
- **Kayak Rentals**: Typically around $12 per hour or $45 for a full day.

Activities

- **Snorkeling and Diving**: Explore the park's coral reefs and underwater marine life, accessible from the shore or by boat tours.
- **Kayaking and Paddleboarding**: Rent kayaks or paddleboards to navigate the park's tranquil waters and mangrove trails.
- **Fishing**: Designated fishing areas provide opportunities to

catch a variety of saltwater fish species.

Facilities

- **Visitor Center**: Offers information about the park, exhibits on local wildlife, and educational materials.
- **Campgrounds**: Several camping areas, including beachfront sites and cabins, are available with amenities such as restrooms, showers, and picnic tables.
- **Concession Stand**: Sells snacks, beverages, and rental equipment for water activities.

Trails and Activities

- **Nature Trails**: Short trails, such as the Silver Palm Trail, provide scenic views of the island's flora and fauna, including rare plant species and birdwatching opportunities.
- **Guided Tours**: Park rangers occasionally offer guided tours and educational programs focusing on the park's ecology and history.

Visitor Tips

- **Advance Reservations**: Camping sites and cabins are highly popular and should be reserved well in advance, especially during peak seasons.
- **Protective Gear**: Bring reef-safe sunscreen, hats, and sunglasses to protect against the intense Florida sun.
- **Water Safety**: Always wear a life jacket when engaging in water activities and be aware of local tide and weather conditions.

- **Respect Wildlife**: Do not disturb or feed wildlife. Observe from a distance to ensure the safety and health of both the animals and yourself.
- **Pack Essentials**: Bring plenty of water, snacks, and any necessary equipment for a comfortable visit, as the park is relatively remote with limited nearby services.

Bahia Honda State Park offers a perfect blend of natural beauty and recreational activities, making it an ideal destination for those seeking a serene escape into the pristine environment of the Florida Keys.

Outdoor Activities and Adventures

Southern Florida is a haven for outdoor enthusiasts, offering a diverse range of activities and adventures that take full advantage of its unique landscapes, warm climate, and abundant wildlife. Whether you're exploring the expansive Everglades, diving into the vibrant coral reefs, or enjoying the pristine beaches, Southern Florida provides countless opportunities for adventure.

1. **Water-Based Activities**
   a. Snorkeling and Scuba Diving

- **Locations**: John Pennekamp Coral Reef State Park, Biscayne National Park, Dry Tortugas National Park
- **Highlights**: Explore the vibrant coral reefs teeming with marine life such as tropical fish, sea turtles, and rays.

Notable sites include the Christ of the Abyss statue and the shipwrecks within the Florida Keys National Marine Sanctuary.
- **Tips**: Ensure you have the appropriate gear and check local regulations for permits and safety guidelines.

b. Kayaking and Canoeing

- **Locations**: Oleta River State Park, Everglades National Park, Bahia Honda State Park
- **Highlights**: Paddle through serene mangrove forests, navigate coastal waterways, and explore hidden coves. The Oleta River offers a mix of open water and mangrove trails, while the Everglades provide a unique experience through its vast wetlands.
- **Tips**: Rent equipment from local outfitters and consider guided tours for a more informative experience.

c. Fishing

- **Locations**: Florida Bay, Biscayne Bay, Ten Thousand Islands
- **Highlights**: Southern Florida is a world-class fishing destination with opportunities for both saltwater and freshwater fishing. Target species include tarpon, snook, redfish, and bonefish.
- **Tips**: Obtain the necessary fishing licenses and familiarize yourself with local regulations to protect fish populations and habitats.

2. Hiking and Nature Trails
a. Hiking in the Everglades

- **Locations**: Anhinga Trail, Shark Valley, Gumbo Limbo Trail
- **Highlights**: Experience the unique ecosystems of the Everglades on well-maintained trails that offer excellent wildlife viewing opportunities. The Anhinga Trail is famous for its abundance of birds and alligators.
- **Tips**: Wear comfortable, waterproof shoes, and bring insect repellent, especially during the wet season.

b. Coastal and Inland Trails

- **Locations**: Bahia Honda State Park, Big Cypress National Preserve, Jonathan Dickinson State Park
- **Highlights**: Walk along scenic coastal trails with breathtaking ocean views or venture into inland trails that showcase Florida's diverse flora and fauna. Big Cypress offers a mix of swamp and prairie landscapes, while Jonathan Dickinson features varied terrain and historic sites.
- **Tips**: Carry plenty of water, a hat, and sunscreen to stay protected from the sun.

3. Cycling and Mountain Biking
a. Off-Road Biking

- **Locations**: Oleta River State Park, Markham Park, Amelia Earhart Park
- **Highlights**: Enjoy challenging off-road biking trails that cater to various skill levels. Oleta River State Park offers over 15 miles of trails winding through natural landscapes, while Markham Park features technical courses for advanced riders.
- **Tips**: Ensure your bike is in good condition and wear

appropriate safety gear, including a helmet and pads.

b. Road Cycling

- **Locations**: Overseas Heritage Trail, Shark Valley Trail
- **Highlights**: Ride along scenic routes with picturesque views of the coastline and natural surroundings. The Overseas Heritage Trail runs parallel to the Florida Keys, providing a unique cycling experience over historic bridges and through charming towns.
- **Tips**: Plan your route in advance, bring a repair kit, and adhere to traffic regulations.

4. Wildlife Viewing and Birdwatching
a. Everglades National Park

- **Highlights**: Spot a diverse array of wildlife, including alligators, manatees, and over 350 species of birds. The park is a designated Wetland of International Importance and offers numerous observation points and guided tours.
- **Tips**: Early morning or late afternoon are the best times for wildlife viewing. Bring binoculars and a field guide to enhance your experience.

b. Coastal Birdwatching

- **Locations**: Ding Darling National Wildlife Refuge, Merritt Island National Wildlife Refuge
- **Highlights**: These refuges are renowned for their birdwatching opportunities, with habitats ranging from mangroves to coastal marshes. Look for species such as roseate

spoonbills, pelicans, and ospreys.
- **Tips**: Visit during migratory seasons for the best birdwatching opportunities and stay quiet to avoid disturbing the wildlife.

5. Camping and Backcountry Adventures
a. Frontcountry Camping

- **Locations**: Bahia Honda State Park, Long Key State Park, Flamingo Campground (Everglades)
- **Highlights**: Enjoy the amenities of developed campgrounds with easy access to beaches, trails, and water activities. Bahia Honda offers oceanfront campsites with stunning sunrise views.
- **Tips**: Make reservations well in advance, especially during peak seasons, and be prepared for mosquitoes and other insects.

b. Backcountry Camping

- **Locations**: Everglades National Park, Big Cypress National Preserve
- **Highlights**: For a more rugged experience, explore backcountry camping in the remote areas of the Everglades or Big Cypress. These areas provide solitude and a deeper connection with nature.
- **Tips**: Obtain the necessary permits, pack essential gear for wilderness survival, and follow Leave No Trace principles to minimize your impact on the environment.

Southern Florida's diverse outdoor activities cater to all interests and skill levels, making it an ideal destination for adventure seekers and nature lovers. Whether you're exploring the depths of coral reefs, navigating the winding trails of mangrove forests, or observing the rich wildlife, the region promises unforgettable experiences in the great outdoors.

Accommodation Options in Southern Florida

Southern Florida offers a variety of accommodation options ranging from luxury resorts to campgrounds, each providing unique experiences and access to the region's natural and cultural attractions. Here's a detailed guide to some of the best places to stay, their prices, nearby attractions, and tips for visitors:

1. **The Ritz-Carlton Key Biscayne**
   Location: 455 Grand Bay Dr, Key Biscayne, FL 33149
   Prices: Starting around $500 per night
   Side Attractions:

   - **Bill Baggs Cape Florida State Park**: Explore historic lighthouse tours, hiking, and picnicking.
   - **Miami Seaquarium**: Enjoy marine life exhibits and shows.
   - **Crandon Park**: Offers golf, tennis, and beautiful beaches.

Guide Tips:

- **Reservations**: Book well in advance, especially during peak season.

- **Dining**: Take advantage of the on-site fine dining options and nearby seafood restaurants.
- **Activities**: Utilize the resort's recreational activities, including water sports and spa services.

2. **Cheeca Lodge & Spa**
   Location: 81801 Overseas Hwy, Islamorada, FL 33036
   Prices: Starting around $350 per night
   Side Attractions:

- **Islamorada Dive Center**: Ideal for snorkeling and diving excursions.
- **Theater of the Sea**: Marine park with dolphin and sea lion shows.
- **Indian Key Historic State Park**: Accessible by kayak for historical site exploration.

Guide Tips:

- **Water Activities**: Book fishing charters and water sport rentals through the resort.
- **Relaxation**: Take advantage of the full-service spa for a relaxing experience.
- **Nature**: Visit nearby parks and preserves for a taste of the local ecosystem.

3. **Flamingo Campground, Everglades National Park**
   Location: 1 Flamingo Lodge Highway, Homestead, FL 33034
   Prices: Tent sites around $20 per night, RV sites around $30 per night
   Side Attractions:

- **Anhinga Trail**: Famous for wildlife viewing, including alligators and birds.
- **Shark Valley**: Offers tram tours and a 15-mile bike trail.
- **Eco Pond**: Great for birdwatching and observing other wildlife.

Guide Tips:

- **Reservations**: Reserve campsites well in advance, especially during winter months.
- **Preparedness**: Bring insect repellent and prepare for changing weather conditions.
- **Activities**: Participate in ranger-led programs and guided tours for an educational experience.

4. **Casa Morada**
   Location: 136 Madeira Rd, Islamorada, FL 33036
   Prices: Starting around $300 per night
   Side Attractions:

- **Lignumvitae Key Botanical State Park**: Accessible by boat, offers guided tours.
- **Windley Key Fossil Reef Geological State Park**: Features trails and fossilized coral.
- **Founders Park**: Offers recreational facilities and a beautiful beach.

Guide Tips:

- **Tranquility**: Perfect for a quiet and intimate getaway, ideal for couples.

- **Boating**: Use the resort's boating facilities to explore nearby keys.
- **Local Cuisine**: Dine at local restaurants to experience fresh seafood and local flavors.

5. **Long Key State Park Campground**
   Location: 67400 Overseas Hwy, Long Key, FL 33001
   Prices: Around $36 per night
   Side Attractions:

- **Long Key State Park**: Offers hiking trails, kayaking, and birdwatching.
- **Robbie's of Islamorada**: Feed tarpon and enjoy waterfront dining.
- **Key West**: A day trip to this vibrant town offers historic sites, shopping, and nightlife.

Guide Tips:

- **Waterfront Sites**: Book early to secure waterfront sites with beautiful sunrise views.
- **Kayaking**: Rent kayaks to explore the park's marine life and mangroves.
- **Packing**: Bring all necessary camping gear and supplies, as facilities are basic.

6. **The Breakers Palm Beach**
   Location: 1 S County Rd, Palm Beach, FL 33480
   Prices: Starting around $600 per night
   Side Attractions:

- **Worth Avenue**: Luxury shopping and dining.
- **Flagler Museum**: Historic mansion turned museum.
- **Norton Museum of Art**: Offers a diverse collection of art exhibits.

Guide Tips:

- **Luxury Experience**: Indulge in the resort's amenities, including world-class dining and a private beach.
- **Cultural Sites**: Explore nearby cultural attractions and historic sites.
- **Golf and Tennis**: Take advantage of the resort's top-rated golf courses and tennis courts.

General Guide Tips for Southern Florida Visitors

- **Booking in Advance**: Especially for popular resorts and campgrounds, advance reservations are essential.
- **Weather Preparation**: Pack for warm weather and sudden rain showers; lightweight, breathable clothing is ideal.
- **Insect Protection**: Mosquitoes can be prevalent, especially in the Everglades; insect repellent is a must.
- **Local Cuisine**: Don't miss out on trying fresh seafood and local specialties such as Key lime pie.
- **Respect Nature**: Follow Leave No Trace principles in natural areas, especially in protected parks and preserves.

Southern Florida's diverse accommodation options cater to all types of travelers, from luxury seekers to nature enthusiasts, ensuring a memorable and comfortable stay amidst some of the most beautiful landscapes in the United States.

CHAPTER 3

Local Flora and Fauna

Southern Florida is a biodiversity hotspot, boasting a rich array of flora and fauna thanks to its unique blend of tropical and subtropical climates, coastal ecosystems, and extensive wetlands. This region supports a wide variety of plant and animal species, many of which are found nowhere else in the United States.

Flora

Southern Florida's flora includes a diverse mix of native plants adapted to its warm, humid environment. Here are some of the key plant species and ecosystems:

1. **Mangroves**

- **Red Mangrove (Rhizophora mangle)**: Known for its distinctive prop roots, red mangroves thrive along coastal areas and provide critical habitat for fish, birds, and other wildlife.
- **Black Mangrove (Avicennia germinans)**: Identified by their pneumatophores (aerial roots), black mangroves are often found in slightly higher elevations than red mangroves.
- **White Mangrove (Laguncularia racemosa)**: Typically found even further inland, these mangroves have rounded leaves and specialized glands for excreting salt.

1. **Seagrasses**

- **Turtle Grass (Thalassia testudinum)**: A dominant seagrass species in Florida's coastal waters, providing essential habitat and food for marine life such as sea turtles.

- **Manatee Grass (Syringodium filiforme)**: Recognizable by its cylindrical blades, it supports a variety of marine species, including the manatee, which feeds on it.

1. **Everglades Flora**

- **Sawgrass (Cladium jamaicense)**: The iconic plant of the Everglades, forming dense stands that dominate the landscape.
- **Cypress Trees (Taxodium distichum)**: Found in freshwater swamps and along rivers, these trees are notable for their buttressed trunks and "knees," which are thought to help with oxygen exchange in waterlogged soils.
- **Periphyton**: A complex mixture of algae, cyanobacteria, microbes, and detritus that forms the basis of the food web in the Everglades.

1. **Hardwood Hammocks**

- **Live Oak (Quercus virginiana)**: A dominant tree species in hardwood hammocks, known for its sprawling branches and resilience.
- **Gumbo Limbo (Bursera simaruba)**: Often called the "tourist tree" for its red, peeling bark, this tree is common in hammocks and coastal areas.
- **Strangler Fig (Ficus aurea)**: This tree starts as an epiphyte and eventually envelops its host, creating a dense canopy.

Fauna

Southern Florida's fauna is equally diverse, with numerous species that are iconic to the region:

1. **Birds**

- **Roseate Spoonbill (Platalea ajaja)**: Recognizable by its bright pink plumage and spoon-shaped bill, found in wetlands and coastal areas.
- **Wood Stork (Mycteria americana)**: A large wading bird often seen in the Everglades, important as an indicator species for wetland health.
- **Snail Kite (Rostrhamus sociabilis)**: A raptor that feeds almost exclusively on apple snails, found in the Everglades and other wetlands.

1. **Reptiles and Amphibians**

- **American Alligator (Alligator mississippiensis)**: A keystone species in the Everglades, playing a critical role in maintaining the ecosystem.
- **American Crocodile (Crocodylus acutus)**: Found in coastal areas and brackish waters, this species is more elusive and rarer than the alligator.
- **Green Tree Frog (Hyla cinerea)**: Common in wetlands and hammocks, this bright green frog is easily recognizable and often heard calling at night.

1. **Mammals**

- **Florida Panther (Puma concolor coryi)**: A critically endangered subspecies of cougar, found in the remote wilderness areas of Southern Florida.
- **West Indian Manatee (Trichechus manatus)**: These gentle giants frequent coastal waters, rivers, and springs, feeding

on seagrass and other aquatic vegetation.
- **Raccoon (Procyon lotor)**: Adaptable and common, raccoons are found in various habitats, including urban areas.

1. **Marine Life**

- **Loggerhead Sea Turtle (Caretta caretta)**: A threatened species that nests on Southern Florida beaches, with major nesting sites in the region.
- **Spotted Eagle Ray (Aetobatus narinari)**: Often seen gliding through the clear waters of the Florida Keys and coastal areas.
- **Bottlenose Dolphin (Tursiops truncatus)**: Frequently spotted in coastal waters and bays, these intelligent marine mammals are a favorite among wildlife watchers.

Conservation Efforts

Efforts to conserve Southern Florida's unique flora and fauna are ongoing, with numerous initiatives in place to protect these natural resources:

- **Everglades Restoration**: A comprehensive plan to restore the natural flow of water through the Everglades, benefiting both plant and animal species.
- **Protected Areas**: Numerous state parks, national parks, and wildlife refuges provide safe havens for wildlife and preserve critical habitats.
- **Species Recovery Programs**: Focused efforts to protect endangered species such as the Florida panther, manatee, and American crocodile through habitat protection, captive breeding, and public education.

CHAPTER 3

Visitor Tips

- **Respect Wildlife**: Observe animals from a distance, never feed wildlife, and follow all park guidelines to ensure minimal impact on natural habitats.
- **Stay on Trails**: Stick to designated trails to protect sensitive vegetation and reduce the risk of disturbing wildlife.
- **Use Reef-Safe Sunscreen**: If participating in water activities, use sunscreen that doesn't harm coral reefs and marine life.
- **Educate Yourself**: Learn about the local ecosystems and species before visiting, enhancing your appreciation and understanding of the area's natural heritage.

Southern Florida's rich tapestry of flora and fauna makes it a remarkable destination for nature enthusiasts, offering endless opportunities for exploration and discovery.

Chapter 4

COASTAL FLORIDA

Coastal Florida, with its extensive shoreline stretching along both the Atlantic Ocean and the Gulf of Mexico, is a region of unparalleled natural beauty and ecological diversity. This area is renowned for its pristine beaches, vibrant coral reefs, and abundant marine life, making it a magnet for tourists and nature enthusiasts alike. The coastline features a mix of bustling cities, quaint seaside towns, and protected natural areas, each offering a unique glimpse into Florida's coastal charm. The Atlantic coast, characterized by its long sandy beaches and lively surf, includes famous destinations such as Miami Beach, Fort Lauderdale, and Daytona Beach. These areas are not only popular for their sunbathing and swimming opportunities but also for water sports like surfing, kiteboarding, and deep-sea fishing. The Gulf Coast, with its calmer waters and barrier islands, offers a different experience, with destinations like Clearwater, Sarasota, and the idyllic

Florida Keys. Here, visitors can enjoy snorkeling, kayaking through mangroves, and exploring the vibrant underwater ecosystems teeming with colorful coral and diverse marine species.

The coastal environment is home to a rich array of wildlife, including manatees, sea turtles, and a myriad of bird species that inhabit the coastal marshes, estuaries, and mangrove forests. Conservation efforts are paramount in this region, with numerous wildlife refuges, state parks, and marine sanctuaries dedicated to preserving these critical habitats and the species that depend on them. Coastal Florida is also steeped in history, with landmarks like the Castillo de San Marcos in St. Augustine, the oldest masonry fort in the continental United States, and the historic lighthouses dotting the coastline, each with its own story to tell.

Moreover, the coastal communities are vibrant with cultural events, seafood festivals, and a rich maritime heritage that reflects the deep connection between the people and the sea. From the cosmopolitan vibe of Miami, with its rich blend of cultures and cuisines, to the laid-back atmosphere of the Gulf Islands, Coastal Florida offers a diverse and dynamic experience. Whether you're exploring the mangrove tunnels of the Everglades, diving into the clear waters of the Dry Tortugas, or simply relaxing on a sandy beach watching a breathtaking sunset, Coastal Florida promises an unforgettable adventure that captures the essence of the Sunshine State.

Honeymoon Island State Park

Honeymoon Island State Park is a beautiful barrier island located on the Gulf Coast of Florida, known for its pristine beaches, crystal-clear waters, and diverse natural habitats. The park spans approximately 2,810 acres, offering visitors a perfect blend of recreational activities, scenic trails, and wildlife viewing opportunities.

Location

- **Address**: 1 Causeway Blvd, Dunedin, FL 34698
- **GPS Coordinates**: 28.0644° N, 82.8260° W
- **Directions**: Honeymoon Island State Park is accessible via the Dunedin Causeway, which connects the island to the mainland. It is located just west of Dunedin and is approximately a 40-minute drive from Tampa.

Trail Features

Honeymoon Island State Park features several well-maintained trails that allow visitors to explore its diverse ecosystems, including pine forests, mangrove swamps, and coastal dunes.

1. Osprey Trail

- **Length**: Approximately 2.5 miles (round trip)
- **Features**: This trail winds through a pine flatwood forest, offering excellent opportunities to see a variety of bird species, including the park's namesake osprey, as well as bald eagles and great horned owls. The trail is relatively flat

and easy to navigate, making it suitable for all fitness levels.
- **Wildlife**: Besides birds, visitors might spot gopher tortoises, armadillos, and various reptiles along the trail.

1. **Pelican Cove Trail**

- **Length**: Approximately 1.5 miles (round trip)
- **Features**: This shorter trail leads to a secluded cove and offers beautiful views of the surrounding waters. It is ideal for those looking for a peaceful walk and a chance to observe the park's coastal habitats.

1. **Nature Center Boardwalk**

- **Length**: Approximately 0.5 miles
- **Features**: This boardwalk trail provides an accessible route through a mangrove swamp, offering an educational experience about the importance of these ecosystems. It is suitable for all visitors, including those with mobility challenges.

Side Attractions

1. **Beaches**

- Honeymoon Island is renowned for its stunning, white-sand beaches. Visitors can enjoy sunbathing, swimming, and shelling. The beaches are also great spots for beachcombing, with a variety of shells and marine life often washing ashore.

1. **Rotary Centennial Nature Center**

- This educational facility offers exhibits on the island's natural and cultural history, as well as interactive displays about local wildlife and habitats. It's a great place to learn more about the park's ecology before heading out to explore.

1. **Paddling and Kayaking**

- The park provides access to calm waters perfect for kayaking and paddleboarding. Rentals are available on-site, and guided tours can be arranged for those interested in exploring the mangroves and nearby waters.

1. **Fishing**

- Anglers can enjoy fishing from the shoreline or from boats. Common catches include snook, redfish, and sea trout. Fishing is a popular activity on the island, and there are designated fishing areas to ensure the best experience.

Guide Tips for Visitors

1. **Best Time to Visit**: Early morning or late afternoon is ideal for birdwatching and avoiding the midday heat. The park is open year-round, but the cooler months from October to April are particularly pleasant.
2. **Wildlife Etiquette**: Maintain a respectful distance from all wildlife, especially nesting birds and sea turtles. Do not feed or disturb any animals, and always follow park guidelines to protect the natural habitat.
3. **Beach Safety**: The Gulf waters can have strong currents. Always swim in designated areas and heed any warning

flags or advisories. Sunscreen and plenty of water are essential for a safe and enjoyable beach day.
4. **Trail Preparation**: Wear comfortable, sturdy shoes for hiking. Carry water, insect repellent, and a hat for sun protection. Binoculars and a camera are great for wildlife viewing and photography.
5. **Facilities**: The park has picnic areas, restrooms, and a café near the main beach area. Plan to bring a picnic lunch and enjoy a meal with a view, or visit the café for refreshments.
6. **Conservation Awareness**: Follow the Leave No Trace principles by taking all trash with you, staying on designated trails, and respecting the park's natural and cultural resources.

Honeymoon Island State Park offers a perfect blend of relaxation and adventure, with its pristine natural landscapes, abundant wildlife, and range of outdoor activities. Whether you're exploring the trails, enjoying a day at the beach, or learning about local ecology at the nature center, this park provides a memorable experience for all visitors.

Caladesi Island State Park

Caladesi Island State Park, one of Florida's few remaining undeveloped barrier islands, offers a pristine natural environment perfect for outdoor enthusiasts and nature lovers. The park is renowned for its untouched beaches, lush mangroves, and diverse wildlife, making it a perfect destination for a day trip or a longer stay.

Location

- **Address**: 1 Causeway Blvd, Dunedin, FL 34698
- **GPS Coordinates**: 28.0328° N, 82.8196° W
- **Directions**: Caladesi Island is accessible primarily by boat. Visitors can take a ferry from Honeymoon Island State Park or arrive by private boat or kayak. The ferry departs from the marina at Honeymoon Island State Park, which is located off the Dunedin Causeway.

Trail Features

Caladesi Island State Park offers several trails that allow visitors to explore its diverse ecosystems, from maritime forests to sandy shores.

1. **Island Trail**

- **Length**: Approximately 3 miles (round trip)
- **Features**: This loop trail winds through a variety of habitats, including pine flatwoods, oak hammocks, and mangrove swamps. Interpretive signs along the trail provide information about the island's flora and fauna.
- **Wildlife**: The trail offers opportunities to see gopher tortoises, armadillos, and various bird species such as herons, egrets, and osprey.

1. **Beach Walk**

- **Length**: Variable, depending on your chosen path along the shoreline
- **Features**: A stroll along the park's beautiful beaches is a

must. The soft, white sand and clear Gulf waters provide a picturesque setting. Beachcombers can find an array of shells and occasionally spot dolphins swimming offshore.

Side Attractions

1. **Beaches**

- Caladesi Island's beaches are consistently rated among the best in the United States. The unspoiled sandy shores are perfect for sunbathing, swimming, and picnicking. The beach also provides excellent opportunities for shelling.

1. **Mangrove Kayak Trail**

- Rent a kayak from the park's concession stand and paddle through the mangrove tunnels. This unique experience allows you to explore the island's mangrove ecosystem up close, with the chance to see fish, crabs, and various bird species.

1. **Fishing**

- Anglers can fish from the shore or from their boats. Common catches include snook, redfish, and sea trout. The calm, clear waters around the island are ideal for both novice and experienced fishers.

1. **Picnic Areas**

- The park has several picnic pavilions equipped with tables and grills, providing a perfect spot for a family meal with a view of the Gulf of Mexico.

Guide Tips for Visitors

1. **Best Time to Visit**: Early mornings and weekdays are less crowded, providing a more peaceful experience. The park is open year-round, but visiting during the cooler months (October to April) can be particularly pleasant.
2. **Ferry Information**: The ferry service from Honeymoon Island State Park runs several times daily, with tickets available for purchase at the marina. It's recommended to arrive early, especially during peak seasons, as the ferry can fill up quickly.
3. **Water and Sun Protection**: Bring plenty of water, sunscreen, and a hat to protect yourself from the sun. The island has limited shade, especially on the beaches, so staying hydrated and protected is crucial.
4. **Wildlife Viewing**: Bring binoculars and a camera for birdwatching and wildlife photography. Keep a respectful distance from all wildlife and do not feed any animals.
5. **Insect Repellent**: Insect repellent is recommended, especially if you plan to hike the trails or paddle through the mangroves. Mosquitoes and other insects can be prevalent, particularly in warmer months.
6. **Facilities**: The park has restrooms and showers near the marina, making it convenient for day-trippers to freshen up before heading back. There is also a small snack bar and gift shop.
7. **Conservation Awareness**: Follow Leave No Trace principles by taking all trash with you, staying on designated

trails, and respecting the park's natural resources. Protect the delicate ecosystems by not disturbing wildlife or removing shells and plants.
8. **Boating Tips**: If arriving by private boat, be aware of the designated anchoring areas and respect the protected seagrass beds. Avoid speeding near the island to protect marine life, including manatees.

Caladesi Island State Park is a gem of Florida's Gulf Coast, offering a serene escape with its untouched natural beauty and wealth of outdoor activities. Whether you're hiking through the island's diverse trails, kayaking the mangrove-lined waters, or simply relaxing on the stunning beaches, Caladesi Island provides a memorable and tranquil experience for all visitors.

Sebastian Inlet State Park

Sebastian Inlet State Park is a popular destination located on Florida's east coast, known for its excellent fishing, surfing, and diverse natural habitats. The park spans over 1,000 acres and provides a variety of recreational opportunities, from hiking and birdwatching to beachcombing and camping.

Location

- **Address**: 9700 S Highway A1A, Melbourne Beach, FL 32951
- **GPS Coordinates**: 27.8616° N, 80.4460° W
- **Directions**: Sebastian Inlet State Park is located on State Road A1A, approximately 15 miles south of Melbourne Beach

and 15 miles north of Vero Beach. It is easily accessible by car, with well-marked entrances on both the north and south sides of the inlet.

Trail Features

Sebastian Inlet State Park features several trails that showcase the area's unique coastal and wetland ecosystems.

1. **Hammock Trail**

- **Length**: Approximately 1 mile (loop)
- **Features**: This trail meanders through a coastal maritime hammock, offering shade from the canopy of live oaks, saw palmettos, and other native vegetation. Interpretive signs along the trail provide information about the local flora and fauna.
- **Wildlife**: Hikers may spot gopher tortoises, various bird species, and occasionally white-tailed deer.

1. **Sebastian Inlet Marina Loop**

- **Length**: Approximately 1.5 miles (loop)
- **Features**: This trail offers scenic views of the inlet and the Indian River Lagoon. It's a great spot for birdwatching, especially during migratory seasons.
- **Wildlife**: Common sightings include ospreys, pelicans, and wading birds. The lagoon waters are also home to dolphins and manatees.

1. **Beach Walk**

- **Length**: Variable, depending on the chosen path along the shoreline
- **Features**: A walk along the park's beaches provides opportunities for shelling, beachcombing, and enjoying the Atlantic Ocean's waves. The beach is popular for surfing and swimming.

Side Attractions

1. Fishing

- **Sebastian Inlet Bridge**: Known as one of the best fishing spots on Florida's east coast, the inlet is famous for its abundance of snook, redfish, and other saltwater species. The bridge offers a prime location for both day and night fishing.
- **Fishing Pier**: The park has two jetties that extend into the Atlantic Ocean, providing excellent spots for fishing and stunning ocean views.

1. Surfing

- Sebastian Inlet is a renowned surfing destination, attracting surfers from around the world. The waves are consistent and can reach impressive heights, especially during the winter months.

1. McLarty Treasure Museum

- Located within the park, this museum showcases the history of the 1715 Spanish treasure fleet that wrecked off the coast.

It features artifacts recovered from the wrecks and provides a fascinating glimpse into Florida's maritime history.

1. **Sebastian Fishing Museum**

- This museum highlights the history of the area's fishing industry, with exhibits on local fish species, traditional fishing techniques, and the lives of early settlers.

1. **Boating and Kayaking**

- The park offers boat ramps and access to both the Indian River Lagoon and the Atlantic Ocean, making it a popular spot for boating, kayaking, and canoeing.

1. **Camping**

- The park has a full-facility campground with 51 sites that accommodate tents and RVs. The campsites are equipped with water and electricity, and there are restrooms and showers available.

Guide Tips for Visitors

1. **Best Time to Visit**: The park is open year-round, but the cooler months from October to April are particularly pleasant. Early mornings and weekdays tend to be less crowded, providing a more serene experience.
2. **Fishing Regulations**: Make sure to check the latest fishing regulations and obtain the necessary licenses. The park staff can provide information on seasonal closures and

catch limits.
3. **Surfing Safety**: For surfing enthusiasts, it's important to check local surf reports and tide charts. Be aware of rip currents and always surf with a buddy.
4. **Wildlife Etiquette**: Maintain a respectful distance from all wildlife, especially nesting birds and sea turtles. Do not feed or disturb any animals, and follow all park guidelines to protect the natural habitat.
5. **Trail Preparation**: Wear comfortable, sturdy shoes for hiking. Carry water, insect repellent, and a hat for sun protection. Binoculars and a camera are great for wildlife viewing and photography.
6. **Beach Safety**: Swim in designated areas and heed any warning flags or advisories. Sunscreen and plenty of water are essential for a safe and enjoyable beach day.
7. **Museum Visits**: Take the time to visit the McLarty Treasure Museum and the Sebastian Fishing Museum to enrich your understanding of the area's history and culture.
8. **Boating Tips**: If arriving by boat, be aware of the designated anchoring areas and respect the protected seagrass beds. Avoid speeding near the inlet to protect marine life, including manatees.
9. **Conservation Awareness**: Follow Leave No Trace principles by taking all trash with you, staying on designated trails, and respecting the park's natural and cultural resources.

Sebastian Inlet State Park is a treasure trove of natural beauty and recreational opportunities, offering visitors a chance to experience Florida's east coast at its best. Whether you're fishing, surfing, hiking, or simply relaxing on the beach, this park provides a diverse and memorable outdoor experience.

Accommodation Options In Coastal Florida

1. The Ritz-Carlton, Amelia Island

- **Location**: 4750 Amelia Island Parkway, Amelia Island, FL 32034
- **Prices**: Rooms start at around $400 per night, with suites and oceanfront views costing more.
- **Side Attractions**: Nearby attractions include Fort Clinch State Park, Amelia Island Historic District, and the island's beautiful beaches. The hotel offers an 18-hole golf course, a luxury spa, and multiple dining options.
- **Guide Tips for Visitors**:
- Book in advance, especially during peak seasons like spring and summer.
- Take advantage of the hotel's beach equipment rentals and guided nature tours.
- Explore the historic downtown area for local shops, restaurants, and art galleries.

2. Casa Marina Hotel & Restaurant, Jacksonville Beach

- **Location**: 691 1st St N, Jacksonville Beach, FL 32250
- **Prices**: Rates start at approximately $150 per night.
- **Side Attractions**: The hotel is close to Jacksonville Beach Pier, Adventure Landing, and the Beaches Museum & History Park. The beachfront location provides easy access to

water sports and beach activities.
- **Guide Tips for Visitors**:
- Visit the rooftop lounge for panoramic ocean views and live music.
- Take a walk or bike ride along the Jacksonville Beach Boardwalk.
- Try local seafood at nearby restaurants for a taste of the region's culinary offerings.

3. **The Breakers, Palm Beach**

- **Location**: 1 S County Rd, Palm Beach, FL 33480
- **Prices**: Rooms start at around $600 per night.
- **Side Attractions**: Close to Worth Avenue, Flagler Museum, and the Society of the Four Arts. The resort offers multiple pools, a private beach, an 18-hole golf course, and a world-class spa.
- **Guide Tips for Visitors**:
- Make reservations for the hotel's exclusive dining experiences.
- Explore the luxurious shops and boutiques on Worth Avenue.
- Enjoy the resort's complimentary fitness classes and water sports activities.

4. **Cheeca Lodge & Spa, Islamorada**

- **Location**: 81801 Overseas Hwy, Islamorada, FL 33036
- **Prices**: Rates start at approximately $300 per night.
- **Side Attractions**: Located in the Florida Keys, the lodge is near the Theater of the Sea, Islamorada Fish Company, and

Robbie's Marina, where you can feed tarpon. The resort offers fishing charters, water sports, and a nine-hole golf course.
- **Guide Tips for Visitors**:
- Book a fishing charter to experience world-class sport fishing.
- Visit nearby state parks like Indian Key Historic State Park and Lignumvitae Key Botanical State Park.
- Take a sunset cruise for stunning views and photo opportunities.

5. Lido Beach Resort, Sarasota

- **Location**: 700 Ben Franklin Dr, Sarasota, FL 34236
- **Prices**: Rates start at approximately $250 per night.
- **Side Attractions**: Close to St. Armands Circle, Mote Marine Laboratory & Aquarium, and Marie Selby Botanical Gardens. The resort features private beach access, two beachfront pools, and a tiki bar.
- **Guide Tips for Visitors**:
- Explore the shops and restaurants at St. Armands Circle.
- Visit the nearby Ringling Museum of Art for a cultural experience.
- Take a kayak tour through Sarasota Bay to see local wildlife and mangrove tunnels.

6. Ocean Key Resort & Spa, Key West

- **Location**: 0 Duval St, Key West, FL 33040
- **Prices**: Rates start at around $350 per night.
- **Side Attractions**: Located at the foot of historic Duval Street,

close to Mallory Square, Ernest Hemingway Home and Museum, and Fort Zachary Taylor Historic State Park. The resort offers waterfront dining, a full-service spa, and an oceanfront pool.
- **Guide Tips for Visitors**:
- Watch the sunset at Mallory Square, a local tradition.
- Explore the vibrant nightlife and eclectic shops on Duval Street.
- Rent a bike or scooter to tour the island and visit its historical sites.

7. **The Don CeSar, St. Pete Beach**

- **Location**: 3400 Gulf Blvd, St. Pete Beach, FL 33706
- **Prices**: Rooms start at around $300 per night.
- **Side Attractions**: Close to the Dali Museum, Fort De Soto Park, and downtown St. Petersburg. The hotel offers a private beach, two pools, a luxury spa, and multiple dining options.
- **Guide Tips for Visitors**:
- Take a sunset sailboat tour from the marina.
- Visit the nearby arts and culture districts in St. Petersburg.
- Enjoy water sports like paddleboarding and jet skiing directly from the beach.

8. **WaterColor Inn & Resort, Santa Rosa Beach**

- **Location**: 34 Goldenrod Cir, Santa Rosa Beach, FL 32459
- **Prices**: Rates start at approximately $400 per night.
- **Side Attractions**: Located along Scenic Highway 30A, close to Grayton Beach State Park, Seaside, and Point Washington

State Forest. The resort features private beach access, multiple pools, and a variety of outdoor activities.
- **Guide Tips for Visitors**:
- Rent bikes to explore the 30A bike trail and local beach towns.
- Kayak or paddleboard on Western Lake, a coastal dune lake.
- Visit the local farmers market and artisan shops in Seaside.

General Guide Tips for Visitors

1. **Book Early**: Popular coastal destinations fill up quickly, especially during peak travel seasons (spring break, summer, and holidays). Book accommodations well in advance to secure the best rates and availability.
2. **Check for Deals**: Look for special packages or discounts offered by the hotels or through travel websites. Many resorts offer bundled deals that include dining credits, spa treatments, or activity vouchers.
3. **Pack Appropriately**: Florida's coastal climate can be hot and humid. Pack lightweight, breathable clothing, swimwear, sunscreen, hats, and insect repellent. A reusable water bottle is also essential to stay hydrated.
4. **Be Aware of Weather Conditions**: Florida's weather can change rapidly, especially during hurricane season (June to November). Keep an eye on weather forecasts and have a backup plan in case of inclement weather.
5. **Explore Local Cuisine**: Coastal Florida is known for its fresh seafood and diverse culinary scene. Don't miss out on trying local specialties like stone crab, grouper, and Key lime pie.
6. **Respect Wildlife and Natural Areas**: Many coastal areas are

home to protected wildlife and delicate ecosystems. Follow all guidelines for interacting with wildlife and be mindful of your impact on the environment.
7. **Safety First**: Always follow safety instructions for water activities, be aware of rip currents, and swim in designated areas. Keep your valuables secure and be cautious of your surroundings.

Coastal Florida offers a wealth of accommodation options, from luxury resorts to charming beachside hotels, each providing a unique experience. With stunning beaches, rich history, and diverse recreational opportunities, visitors are sure to find the perfect spot for their coastal getaway.

Chapter 5

SPECIAL INTEREST PARKS

Special interest parks are unique and distinct from traditional state or national parks in that they cater to specific themes, activities, or conservation efforts. These parks often focus on preserving and showcasing particular ecosystems, historical sites, or cultural heritage, offering visitors immersive experiences tailored to their interests.

One common type of special interest park is an ecological reserve, which aims to protect fragile ecosystems and biodiversity. These parks may have strict conservation guidelines, limiting visitor access to minimize human impact and preserve natural habitats. Educational programs and guided tours often highlight the importance of environmental stewardship and biodiversity conservation.

Other special interest parks may focus on cultural or historical significance, preserving archaeological sites, historic landmarks, or traditional cultural practices. These parks offer insights into past civilizations, art, architecture, and traditions, providing visitors with a deeper understanding of regional history and heritage.

Adventure and recreational parks cater to adrenaline enthusiasts, offering activities such as rock climbing, zip-lining, or white-water rafting. These parks prioritize outdoor adventure and may provide equipment rentals, guided tours, and safety instructions for visitors.

Overall, special interest parks play a crucial role in both conservation and education, offering unique opportunities for exploration, learning, and recreation tailored to specific interests and passions. Whether you're interested in wildlife conservation, cultural heritage, or outdoor adventure, these parks provide enriching experiences that connect visitors with the natural and cultural diversity of our world

Historical Parks

Historical parks across the United States offer rich insights into the nation's past, preserving significant sites and artifacts that illuminate various aspects of American history. Here's a detailed overview of some notable historical parks, their locations, and main attractions:

1. Colonial National Historical Park, Virginia

- **Location**: Williamsburg, Yorktown, and Jamestown, Virginia
- **Main Attractions**:
- **Jamestown Settlement**: The site of the first permanent English settlement in America in 1607. Explore reconstructed ships, a Powhatan Indian village, and historical exhibits.
- **Historic Jamestowne**: The original site of Jamestown where archaeological excavations continue to uncover artifacts from the early colonial period.
- **Yorktown Battlefield**: Commemorates the decisive battle of the American Revolution. Visit the battlefield, siege lines, and the Yorktown Victory Monument.

2. Gettysburg National Military Park, Pennsylvania

- **Location**: Gettysburg, Pennsylvania
- **Main Attractions**:
- **Gettysburg Battlefield**: Site of the pivotal Civil War battle fought in July 1863. Explore the battlefield with its historic monuments, memorials, and preserved landscapes.
- **Gettysburg National Cemetery**: Where President Abraham Lincoln delivered his famous Gettysburg Address. Visit the Soldiers' National Monument and gravesites of Civil War soldiers.

3. Independence National Historical Park, Pennsylvania

- **Location**: Philadelphia, Pennsylvania
- **Main Attractions**:
- **Independence Hall**: Where the Declaration of Independence and the U.S. Constitution were debated and adopted. Tour

the assembly room and see the Liberty Bell nearby.
- **Congress Hall**: The former seat of the U.S. Congress from 1790 to 1800, where George Washington was inaugurated for his second term as President.
- **Liberty Bell Center**: Exhibits about the history and significance of the Liberty Bell, an enduring symbol of American independence.

4. Harpers Ferry National Historical Park, West Virginia

- **Location**: Harpers Ferry, West Virginia
- **Main Attractions**:
- **Harpers Ferry**: A historic town where the Potomac and Shenandoah Rivers meet. Explore exhibits on John Brown's raid and the town's role in the Civil War.
- **John Brown's Fort**: A key site associated with abolitionist John Brown's raid in 1859, a pivotal event leading to the Civil War.
- **Harpers Ferry National Historical Park Trails**: Scenic hiking trails offering views of the rivers and surrounding Appalachian Mountains.

5. San Antonio Missions National Historical Park, Texas

- **Location**: San Antonio, Texas
- **Main Attractions**:
- **Mission Concepción, Mission San José, Mission San Juan, Mission Espada**: These Spanish colonial missions were established in the 18th century to convert Native Americans to Christianity. Each mission features beautifully preserved churches, living quarters, and grounds.

- **The Espada Aqueduct**: A historic acequia (irrigation canal) and aqueduct built by Spanish settlers in the 18th century, still in use today.

6. Chaco Culture National Historical Park, New Mexico

- **Location**: Nageezi, New Mexico
- **Main Attractions**:
- **Chaco Canyon**: A major center of ancestral Puebloan culture between AD 900 and 1150. Explore massive stone buildings, astronomical alignments, and ancient roads.
- **Pueblo Bonito**: The largest and most extensively excavated Great House in Chaco Canyon, with over 600 rooms and ceremonial chambers.
- **Chetro Ketl and Pueblo del Arroyo**: Other notable Great Houses with intricate masonry and kivas (ceremonial rooms).

7. Boston National Historical Park, Massachusetts

- **Location**: Boston, Massachusetts
- **Main Attractions**:
- **Freedom Trail**: A 2.5-mile walking trail linking 16 historical sites, including the Paul Revere House, Old North Church, and USS Constitution Museum.
- **Bunker Hill Monument**: Commemorates the Battle of Bunker Hill, a significant Revolutionary War battle. Climb to the top for panoramic views of Boston.

These historical parks not only preserve important sites and structures but also offer educational programs, guided tours, and exhibits that bring American history to life. Visitors can explore the events, people, and cultures that shaped the nation, providing a deeper understanding of our shared heritage.

Botanical Gardens

Florida is home to several stunning botanical gardens, each showcasing unique plant species, lush landscapes, and educational experiences. Here's a detailed overview of some notable botanical gardens in Florida, their locations, main attractions, and visitor requirements:

1. Fairchild Tropical Botanic Garden, Coral Gables

- **Location**: 10901 Old Cutler Rd, Coral Gables, FL 33156
- **Main Attractions**:
- **Rainforest**: Walk through a lush tropical rainforest with waterfalls and rare plant species.
- **Butterfly Conservatory**: A tropical paradise filled with colorful butterflies and exotic plants.
- **Rare Plant House**: Houses endangered and rare plant species from around the world.
- **Edible Garden**: Learn about sustainable gardening and taste fresh produce from the garden.
- **Visitor Requirements**: Tickets should be purchased online in advance. Comfortable walking shoes, sunscreen, and water are recommended. Follow guidelines to protect the garden's flora and fauna.

2. Marie Selby Botanical Gardens, Sarasota

- **Location**: 1534 Mound St, Sarasota, FL 34236
- **Main Attractions**:
- **Tropical Conservatory**: Features a diverse collection of orchids, bromeliads, and epiphytes.
- **Historic Spanish Point**: A waterfront archaeological and historical site showcasing native Florida plants.
- **Children's Rainforest Garden**: Interactive exhibits and activities for young visitors to explore tropical plants.
- **Bayside Gardens**: Overlooks Sarasota Bay and includes a mangrove walk and native plant exhibits.
- **Visitor Requirements**: Advance tickets are required. Check for guided tours and special events. Wear comfortable shoes for walking and bring sunscreen and insect repellent.

3. Naples Botanical Garden, Naples

- **Location**: 4820 Bayshore Dr, Naples, FL 34112
- **Main Attractions**:
- **Brazilian Garden**: A lush landscape featuring tropical plants native to Brazil.
- **Asian Garden**: Highlights plants from Asia, including a Thai pavilion and water features.
- **Preserve Trail**: Walk through natural Florida habitats, including wetlands and upland pine forests.
- **Smith Children's Garden**: Interactive play areas and educational exhibits for young visitors.
- **Visitor Requirements**: Purchase tickets online in advance. Wear comfortable attire suitable for walking outdoors. Follow guidelines for protecting the garden's plants and

wildlife.

4. Mounts Botanical Garden, West Palm Beach

- **Location**: 531 N Military Trl, West Palm Beach, FL 33415
- **Main Attractions**:
- **Butterfly Garden**: A favorite spot for butterfly enthusiasts, featuring native and tropical butterfly species.
- **Palm and Cycad Walk**: Explore a collection of palms and cycads from around the world.
- **Herb Garden**: Learn about culinary and medicinal herbs, including tastings and demonstrations.
- **Windows on the Floating World**: A wetland garden showcasing aquatic plants and wildlife.
- **Visitor Requirements**: Tickets can be purchased online or at the gate. Check for seasonal events and workshops. Wear comfortable walking shoes and bring water and sunscreen.

5. McKee Botanical Garden, Vero Beach

- **Location**: 350 US-1, Vero Beach, FL 32962
- **Main Attractions**:
- **Waterlily Garden**: Features a renowned collection of water lilies and aquatic plants.
- **Spanish Kitchen Garden**: Displays plants historically used in Spanish cuisine and gardens.
- **Bamboo Pavilion**: A serene spot surrounded by bamboo groves and tropical foliage.
- **Native Plant Garden**: Showcases Florida's native plants and their importance in local ecosystems.
- **Visitor Requirements**: Purchase tickets in advance. Wear

comfortable attire for walking. Respect the garden's rules on plant conservation and wildlife protection.

Visitor Requirements for Visitation:

- **Advance Tickets**: Purchase tickets online or in advance, especially during peak seasons.
- **Guided Tours and Events**: Check for guided tours, workshops, and educational programs.
- **Conservation Guidelines**: Follow guidelines for protecting plants and wildlife. Avoid picking flowers or disturbing animals.
- **Comfortable Attire**: Wear comfortable walking shoes, weather-appropriate clothing, and bring water, sunscreen, and insect repellent.

Florida's botanical gardens offer not only beautiful landscapes and plant collections but also educational opportunities and a chance to connect with nature. Whether you're a botany enthusiast, a family looking for outdoor activities, or a visitor interested in Florida's diverse ecosystems, these gardens provide memorable experiences for all ages.

Birdwatching Spots

Florida is a paradise for birdwatchers, boasting diverse ecosystems that attract a wide range of bird species throughout the year. Here's a detailed overview of some prime birdwatching spots in Florida, their locations, main attractions, and visitor requirements:

1. Everglades National Park

- **Location**: Southern Florida, various entrances including Homestead and Shark Valley
- **Main Attractions**:
- **Anhinga Trail**: Known for close-up views of alligators, wading birds, and other wildlife.
- **Shark Valley**: Offers tram tours and a 15-mile loop road for birdwatching, with opportunities to see herons, egrets, and raptors.
- **Flamingo Area**: Explore coastal marshes and mangrove forests, home to roseate spoonbills, pelicans, and more.
- **Visitor Requirements**: Park entrance fee required. Bring binoculars, water, sunscreen, and insect repellent. Respect wildlife and follow park regulations for conservation.

2. Dry Tortugas National Park

- **Location**: 70 miles west of Key West, accessible by ferry or seaplane
- **Main Attractions**:
- **Fort Jefferson**: Historic fort with nesting colonies of seabirds including frigatebirds and terns.
- **Garden Key**: Sandy beaches and clear waters attract shorebirds and migratory species.
- **Loggerhead Key**: Visit during migration seasons for sightings of rare and diverse bird species.
- **Visitor Requirements**: Advance reservations for ferry or seaplane required. Bring binoculars, camera, water, and

sunscreen. Follow park rules to protect nesting birds and fragile habitats.

3. Sanibel Island and J.N. "Ding" Darling National Wildlife Refuge

- **Location**: Sanibel Island, southwest Florida
- **Main Attractions**:
- **Wildlife Drive**: Scenic route through wetlands and mangroves, home to over 245 bird species including spoonbills and ibises.
- **Bailey Tract**: Offers shorter trails and boardwalks for close-up birdwatching opportunities.
- **Tarpon Bay Explorers**: Guided tours by tram, kayak, or canoe for birdwatching and wildlife viewing.
- **Visitor Requirements**: Entrance fee for Wildlife Drive. Binoculars, camera, and field guide recommended. Respect refuge regulations for wildlife protection.

4. Merritt Island National Wildlife Refuge

- **Location**: Merritt Island, east central Florida near Titusville
- **Main Attractions**:
- **Black Point Wildlife Drive**: Scenic drive through coastal marshes and impoundments, with opportunities to see waterfowl and shorebirds.
- **Wildlife Observation Towers**: Provides panoramic views of the refuge, ideal for spotting wading birds and raptors.
- **Manatee Observation Deck**: Often frequented by birds like ospreys and herons.
- **Visitor Requirements**: Some areas accessible with daily or

annual passes. Bring binoculars, camera, water, and insect repellent. Follow refuge rules for wildlife conservation and safety.

5. Corkscrew Swamp Sanctuary

- **Location**: Near Naples, southwest Florida
- **Main Attractions**:
- **Boardwalk Loop**: A 2.25-mile boardwalk trail through ancient cypress swamps, with sightings of wood storks, herons, and warblers.
- **Blind Pass**: Viewing platform for observing nesting herons and other waterfowl.
- **Birding Tours**: Guided tours offered seasonally for in-depth birdwatching experiences.
- **Visitor Requirements**: Entrance fee for non-members. Binoculars, camera, and birding checklist recommended. Follow sanctuary guidelines for quiet observation and habitat preservation.

Visitor Requirements for Visitation:

- **Access**: Some locations may require advance reservations or permits, especially during peak seasons.
- **Equipment**: Bring binoculars, camera, field guide, water, sunscreen, and insect repellent.
- **Respect Wildlife**: Observe birds from a distance to avoid disturbing nesting or feeding behaviors.
- **Conservation**: Follow park or refuge rules for habitat preservation and respect wildlife protection guidelines.

Florida's birdwatching spots offer unparalleled opportunities to observe diverse avian species in their natural habitats, making them ideal destinations for both casual bird enthusiasts and avid ornithologists alike. Whether exploring wetlands, coastal areas, or pristine forests, visitors can enjoy memorable birdwatching experiences throughout the state.

Scenic Drives and Hiking Trails

Florida offers a variety of scenic drives and hiking trails that showcase its diverse landscapes and natural beauty. Whether you're interested in coastal vistas, lush forests, or unique ecosystems, there's something for everyone to explore.

Overview

Scenic drives and hiking trails in Florida provide opportunities for outdoor enthusiasts to immerse themselves in nature, discover local flora and fauna, and enjoy breathtaking views.

Activities

- **Hiking**: Explore trails ranging from easy walks to challenging hikes through forests, wetlands, and coastal dunes.
- **Birdwatching**: Many trails and drives offer opportunities to observe diverse bird species, especially during migratory seasons.
- **Photography**: Capture stunning landscapes, wildlife, and unique ecosystems along the routes.
- **Nature Study**: Learn about Florida's natural history, ecol-

ogy, and conservation efforts through interpretive signs and guided tours.

Trails Names and Points of Interest
1. Everglades National Park

- **Scenic Drive**: Loop Road Scenic Drive
- **Overview**: A 24-mile gravel road through pine forests, cypress swamps, and sawgrass marshes.
- **Activities**: Wildlife viewing (alligators, birds), photography.
- **Points of Interest**: Big Cypress National Preserve, Clyde Butcher Gallery.
- **Nearby Attractions**: Shark Valley Visitor Center, Gulf Coast Visitor Center.

2. Big Cypress National Preserve

- **Hiking Trail**: Kirby Storter Roadside Park Boardwalk
- **Overview**: A short boardwalk trail through a cypress swamp with interpretive signs.
- **Activities**: Birdwatching, photography.
- **Points of Interest**: Alligator sightings, native plants.
- **Nearby Attractions**: Loop Road, Fakahatchee Strand Preserve State Park.

3. Gulf Islands National Seashore

- **Scenic Drive**: Santa Rosa Island Drive
- **Overview**: A scenic drive along Santa Rosa Island with views of pristine beaches and sand dunes.
- **Activities**: Beachcombing, swimming, wildlife watching.

- **Points of Interest**: Fort Pickens, Historic Pensacola Village.
- **Nearby Attractions**: Pensacola Beach, Naval Aviation Museum.

4. Anastasia State Park

- **Hiking Trail**: Ancient Dunes Nature Trail
- **Overview**: A loop trail through maritime hammock and ancient dunes.
- **Activities**: Birdwatching, beach access.
- **Points of Interest**: Coquina Quarry, Salt Run.
- **Nearby Attractions**: St. Augustine historic district, Castillo de San Marcos.

5. Myakka River State Park

- **Scenic Drive**: Myakka Drive
- **Overview**: A 7-mile scenic drive through oak-palm hammocks and wetlands.
- **Activities**: Canoeing, wildlife viewing (alligators, birds).
- **Points of Interest**: Myakka River, Birdwalk, Canopy Walkway.
- **Nearby Attractions**: Sarasota, Siesta Key Beach.

Nearby Attractions

- **Cultural Sites**: Explore historic towns, museums, and cultural attractions near scenic routes.
- **Beaches and Coastal Areas**: Enjoy coastal activities such as swimming, snorkeling, and beachcombing.
- **Wildlife Refuges and Parks**: Visit nearby wildlife refuges or

state parks for additional hiking trails and wildlife viewing opportunities.
- **Outdoor Recreation**: Engage in activities like fishing, boating, or kayaking at nearby lakes, rivers, or coastal waters.

These scenic drives and hiking trails in Florida offer a blend of natural beauty, recreational opportunities, and educational experiences, making them ideal destinations for outdoor enthusiasts, families, and nature lovers alike. Whether you're seeking a leisurely drive with picturesque views or an adventurous hike through diverse landscapes, Florida's trails and routes provide memorable experiences throughout the year.

6

Chapter 6

CULINARY OPTIONS

Culinary options in Florida reflect a vibrant tapestry of flavors influenced by diverse cultures, coastal abundance, and a rich agricultural heritage. From fresh seafood along the Gulf Coast to Latin-inspired dishes in Miami and innovative farm-to-table cuisine statewide, Florida offers a culinary journey that caters to every palate.

Coastal cities like Miami and Key West are renowned for their seafood delicacies, including stone crabs, grouper sandwiches, and conch fritters. These dishes highlight the freshness of local catch and the region's maritime traditions. Meanwhile, cities like Orlando and Tampa boast multicultural dining scenes, featuring Cuban sandwiches, Colombian arepas, and Puerto Rican mofongo, reflecting the diverse Hispanic community.

Florida's agricultural bounty is celebrated in its farm-to-table dining experiences, where chefs showcase locally sourced ingredients like citrus fruits, tropical fruits, and fresh vegetables in creative and sustainable dishes. From artisanal cheeses in North Florida to citrus-infused desserts in Central Florida, the state's culinary landscape is as diverse as its ecosystems.

Food festivals and farmers' markets across Florida provide opportunities to sample regional specialties and artisanal products, while craft breweries and wineries offer tastings of locally produced beverages. Whether enjoying a casual beachside seafood shack or a fine dining experience overlooking the Everglades, Florida's culinary options promise a delightful fusion of flavors, culture, and hospitality that embodies the Sunshine State's unique culinary identity.

Picnic Areas and Facilities

Picnic areas in Florida offer a range of facilities and culinary options to enhance outdoor dining experiences. Here's a detailed look at what you can expect, including various culinary contents and potential costs:

Picnic Areas and Facilities in Florida: Detailed Information and Explanations

Florida's picnic areas are nestled in scenic parks, along beaches, and amidst lush natural settings, providing ideal spots for families, friends, and travelers to enjoy outdoor meals and recreational activities.

Facilities

- **Picnic Tables and Shelters**: Most picnic areas are equipped with sturdy tables and shaded shelters, offering comfort and protection from the sun.
- **Grills and Fire Rings**: Some locations provide charcoal grills or fire rings for cooking meals outdoors.
- **Restrooms**: Accessible restroom facilities ensure convenience for visitors.
- **Playgrounds and Sports Facilities**: Many parks feature playgrounds, volleyball courts, and open spaces for recreational activities.

Culinary Contents

- **Seafood**: Enjoy fresh catches like shrimp, fish fillets, and crab cakes grilled on-site.
- **Barbecue**: Indulge in classic barbecue fare such as ribs, chicken, and burgers.
- **Salads and Sides**: Pair main dishes with fresh salads, coleslaw, and fruit platters.
- **Snacks and Beverages**: Pack snacks like chips, salsa, and trail mix, along with refreshing beverages such as lemonade and iced tea.
- **Desserts**: Treat yourself to homemade pies, cookies, or fruit cobblers.

Costs

- **DIY Picnics**: Bring your own food and supplies for a cost-effective outdoor dining experience.

- **Park Entry Fees**: Some parks may require entry fees, typically ranging from $5 to $15 per vehicle, depending on the park and season.
- **Rentals and Amenities**: Optional rental fees for pavilions, grills, and additional amenities may apply, ranging from $25 to $100 depending on the location and duration of use.

Examples of Picnic Areas in Florida

1. Fort De Soto Park, St. Petersburg

- **Facilities**: Shaded picnic tables, grills, restrooms, playgrounds.
- **Culinary Options**: Fresh seafood, barbecue, salads, snacks, beverages.
- **Cost**: $5 park entry fee per vehicle.

2. Blue Spring State Park, Orange City

- **Facilities**: Riverside picnic areas, pavilions, restrooms, playgrounds.
- **Culinary Options**: Barbecue, sandwiches, salads, desserts.
- **Cost**: $6 per vehicle park entry fee.

3. Bill Baggs Cape Florida State Park, Key Biscayne

- **Facilities**: Beachside picnic tables, grills, pavilions, restrooms.
- **Culinary Options**: Seafood, Cuban sandwiches, tropical fruits.
- **Cost**: $8 per vehicle park entry fee.

Visitor Tips

- **Reservations**: Some parks allow reservations for pavilions or group picnic areas; check in advance for availability.
- **Pack Essentials**: Bring sunscreen, insect repellent, and reusable containers for leftovers.
- **Clean-Up**: Leave no trace by properly disposing of trash and cleaning up picnic areas after use.

Florida's picnic areas cater to various tastes and preferences, providing scenic settings and culinary delights that enhance outdoor dining experiences for visitors of all ages. Whether enjoying a beachfront barbecue or a riverside seafood feast, these picnic spots offer memorable moments in the Sunshine State's natural beauty.

On-site Cafes and Restaurants

On-site cafes and restaurants in Florida's parks and attractions offer a variety of culinary experiences, from casual dining options to gourmet cuisine. Here's a detailed look at what you can expect, including different culinary offerings, contents, and potential costs:

On-site Cafes and Restaurants in Florida: Detailed Information and Explanations

Florida's parks, museums, and attractions often feature on-site cafes and restaurants that cater to visitors looking to enjoy a meal or snack during their visit. These establishments provide a range of culinary options, from local specialties to international flavors, in settings that complement the surrounding environment.

Culinary Offerings
 1. **Seafood**

- **Contents**: Fresh catches like grouper sandwiches, shrimp tacos, and seafood platters.
- **Cuisine Style**: Coastal and seafood-centric, highlighting local seafood and flavors.
- **Cost**: Prices typically range from $10 to $25 per dish, depending on the selection and location.

2. **American Classics**

- **Contents**: Burgers, sandwiches, salads, and hearty entrees like grilled chicken and steaks.
- **Cuisine Style**: Comfort food with a focus on quality ingredients and classic flavors.
- **Cost**: Meals range from $8 to $20, with options for sides and beverages at additional costs.

3. **International Cuisine**

- **Contents**: Dishes representing various global cuisines such as Italian pastas, Mexican tacos, and Asian stir-fries.
- **Cuisine Style**: Authentic flavors and recipes from around the world, tailored to suit local tastes.
- **Cost**: Prices vary widely depending on the cuisine type and complexity of dishes, typically ranging from $12 to $30 per

meal.

4. Healthy Options

- **Contents**: Fresh salads, wraps, smoothies, and organic or locally sourced ingredients.
- **Cuisine Style**: Emphasis on nutrition, freshness, and sustainability.
- **Cost**: Meals generally range from $8 to $15, with options for vegetarian and vegan dishes.

Locations and Facilities

- **Facilities**: Many cafes and restaurants offer indoor and outdoor seating options, with scenic views or proximity to attractions.
- **Amenities**: Some locations provide grab-and-go options, picnic areas, and souvenir shops.
- **Accessibility**: Accessible facilities for families, groups, and individuals with dietary restrictions or preferences.

Examples of On-site Cafes and Restaurants in Florida
1. Biscayne National Park Visitor Center Cafe, Homestead

- **Culinary Options**: Seafood specials, salads, sandwiches, and local craft beers.
- **Cost**: Average $15 per meal.

2. The Columbia Restaurant, Ybor City, Tampa

- **Culinary Options**: Spanish and Cuban cuisine including

paella, tapas, and Cuban sandwiches.
- **Cost**: Average $20-$30 per meal.

3. Edison and Ford Winter Estates, Fort Myers

- **Culinary Options**: American classics like burgers, salads, and seasonal specials.
- **Cost**: Average $12-$18 per meal.

Visitor Tips

- **Menu Options**: Check menus online or at the establishment for current offerings and prices.
- **Reservations**: For popular or upscale dining spots, consider making reservations, especially during peak seasons.
- **Park Entry**: Some locations may require park entry fees in addition to meal costs.

On-site cafes and restaurants in Florida provide convenient dining options for visitors, offering a taste of local cuisine and international flavors amidst the state's natural beauty and cultural attractions. Whether enjoying a leisurely meal after exploring a park or sampling regional specialties at a historic site, these dining experiences add to the overall enjoyment of visiting Florida's diverse destinations.

Local Cuisine and Food Festivals

Local cuisine and food festivals in Florida celebrate the state's diverse culinary heritage, featuring a wide array of flavors influenced by regional ingredients and cultural traditions. Here's a detailed exploration of what you can expect, including different culinary offerings, contents, and potential costs:

Local Cuisine and Food Festivals in Florida: Detailed Information and Explanations

Florida's local cuisine is a melting pot of flavors, drawing influences from Caribbean, Latin American, Southern, and Native American culinary traditions. Food festivals across the state showcase these diverse flavors, offering opportunities to indulge in authentic dishes and unique culinary experiences.

Culinary Offerings

1. **Seafood**

- **Contents**: Fresh catches such as stone crabs, grouper, shrimp, and oysters prepared in various styles like grilled, blackened, or fried.
- **Cuisine Style**: Emphasis on freshness and coastal flavors, reflecting Florida's abundant seafood resources.
- **Cost**: Prices vary depending on the seafood type and preparation, typically ranging from $15 to $40 per dish at restaurants or festival stalls.

2. **Cuban Cuisine**

- **Contents**: Cuban sandwiches (Cubanos), picadillo (ground

beef dish), Ropa Vieja (shredded beef), plantains (tostones or maduros), and black beans and rice (Moros y Cristianos).
- **Cuisine Style**: Robust flavors with influences from Spanish, African, and Caribbean cooking traditions.
- **Cost**: Meals range from $8 to $20 per dish, depending on the restaurant or festival vendor.

3. Latin American Flavors

- **Contents**: Arepas (corn cakes), empanadas (stuffed pastries), ceviche (marinated seafood), and traditional dishes like Pernil (roast pork).
- **Cuisine Style**: Vibrant and savory dishes showcasing flavors from countries like Colombia, Venezuela, and Argentina.
- **Cost**: Prices typically range from $10 to $25 per dish, depending on the complexity and ingredients used.

4. Southern Cuisine

- **Contents**: Fried chicken, shrimp and grits, collard greens, cornbread, and pecan pie.
- **Cuisine Style**: Comfort food with influences from African, Native American, and European culinary traditions.
- **Cost**: Meals range from $12 to $30 per dish, depending on the restaurant or festival vendor.

Food Festivals in Florida
1. South Beach Wine & Food Festival, Miami

- **Culinary Offerings**: Celebrity chef tastings, wine pairings, and gourmet dinners.

- **Cost**: Tickets range from $75 for individual events to $500+ for exclusive experiences.

2. **Epcot International Food & Wine Festival, Walt Disney World**

- **Culinary Offerings**: Global marketplaces featuring dishes from around the world, cooking demonstrations, and seminars.
- **Cost**: Admission to Epcot required, with food and beverage prices ranging from $4 to $10 per item.

3. **Key West Seafood Festival, Key West**

- **Culinary Offerings**: Fresh local seafood dishes, live music, and family-friendly activities.
- **Cost**: Admission is typically free, with food and drink prices varying by vendor.

Visitor Tips

- **Plan Ahead**: Check festival schedules and restaurant menus in advance for offerings and pricing.
- **Budget**: Allocate funds for admission fees, food purchases, and optional tastings or events.
- **Explore Local Markets**: Visit farmers' markets or food trucks for affordable and authentic culinary experiences.

Florida's local cuisine and food festivals offer a delicious exploration of the state's cultural diversity and culinary creativity. Whether savoring fresh seafood on the coast, enjoying Cuban specialties in Miami, or indulging in international flavors at a food festival, visitors can experience the vibrant tastes that make Florida a unique culinary destination.

Cooking in the Wild: Campfire Recipes and Tips

Cooking in the wild over a campfire can be a rewarding and enjoyable experience, combining the flavors of outdoor cooking with the adventure of exploring nature. Here's a detailed guide to campfire recipes and tips for cooking in the wild:

Campfire Cooking: Detailed Guide
1. **Essential Equipment and Supplies**

- **Fire Starters**: Bring matches, a lighter, or fire starters for igniting your campfire.
- **Cooking Utensils**: Pack a cast iron skillet, grilling grate, tongs, and a spatula for cooking over the fire.
- **Dutch Oven**: Ideal for slow cooking and baking in a campfire setting.
- **Aluminum Foil**: Useful for wrapping food parcels and cooking delicate items.

2. **Campfire Safety**

- **Location**: Choose a designated fire pit or clear a safe area away from dry grass and overhanging branches.
- **Extinguishing**: Always fully extinguish your fire with water and ensure it's cold to the touch before leaving.

3. Campfire Recipes
Breakfast: Campfire Pancakes

- **Ingredients**: Pancake mix, water, maple syrup, fresh berries.
- **Method**: Mix pancake batter, heat skillet over medium fire, ladle batter onto skillet, flip when bubbles appear, cook until golden brown.

Lunch: Grilled Cheese Sandwiches

- **Ingredients**: Bread, cheese slices, butter.
- **Method**: Butter bread slices, place cheese between slices, wrap in foil, toast over coals until cheese melts and bread is golden.

Dinner: Foil Packet Meals

- **Ingredients**: Sliced potatoes, vegetables, seasoned chicken or fish.
- **Method**: Layer ingredients on foil, fold to seal, cook on coals, flipping halfway, until contents are cooked through.

Dessert: Campfire S'mores

- **Ingredients**: Graham crackers, chocolate squares, marshmallows.
- **Method**: Skewer marshmallow, roast over fire until golden, sandwich between crackers with chocolate, let melt.

4. Tips for Cooking in the Wild

- **Prepare Ingredients**: Pre-cut and season ingredients at home to simplify cooking at the campsite.
- **Use Seasoned Wood**: Dry, seasoned wood burns hotter and cleaner, ideal for cooking.
- **Rotate Food**: Turn food regularly to ensure even cooking and prevent burning.
- **Experiment**: Try new recipes and adapt them based on available ingredients and cooking conditions.

5. **Leave No Trace**

- **Clean Up**: Dispose of trash properly, pack out all waste, and leave the campsite as you found it.
- **Respect Wildlife**: Store food securely and avoid attracting wildlife to your cooking area.

6. **Safety Considerations**

- **Fire Regulations**: Observe local fire regulations and any burn bans that may be in effect.
- **First Aid**: Have a basic first aid kit on hand for minor burns or injuries.

Enjoying Campfire Cooking

Cooking in the wild over a campfire adds a sense of adventure and connection to nature. Whether you're enjoying a hearty breakfast, a satisfying lunch, or a delicious dessert under the stars, campfire cooking offers memorable experiences and flavors that enhance any outdoor adventure. By following safety guidelines and respecting the environment, you can create delicious meals and lasting memories in the great outdoors.

Chapter 7

PRACTICAL INFORMATION

Practical information is vital for travelers, offering essential details that ensure smooth and informed journeys. It encompasses transportation options, accommodation choices, dining recommendations, safety tips, currency exchange, communication tools, cultural norms, and environmental considerations. Understanding these aspects enhances travel planning, facilitating seamless transitions and enriching experiences by promoting preparedness, respect for local customs, and responsible tourism practices. Whether navigating new destinations, enjoying culinary delights, or embracing cultural diversity, practical information empowers travelers to make informed decisions and maximize their enjoyment while fostering positive interactions with local communities and environments.

Park Passes and Fees

Park passes and fees provide access to recreational areas, national parks, and state parks, offering visitors opportunities to explore natural landscapes and participate in outdoor activities. Here's a detailed overview of park passes and fees:

Park Passes
 1. **Annual Passes**

- **Description**: Annual passes offer unlimited access to designated parks for one year from the date of purchase.
- **Benefits**: Cost-effective for frequent visitors, providing access to multiple parks within a region or nationwide.
- **Types**: National Park Annual Pass, State Park Annual Pass, Regional Passes.

2. **Daily Entry Fees**

- **Description**: Entry fees for daily visits vary by park and are typically per vehicle or per person.
- **Benefits**: Allows day-use access to park facilities, trails, and amenities.
- **Variances**: Prices vary based on park popularity, amenities, and conservation efforts.

Fees
 1. **Vehicle Entry**

- **Description**: Charges per vehicle entering the park, encouraging carpooling and reducing congestion.

- **Examples**: Typically range from $5 to $30 per vehicle, depending on park size and popularity.

2. **Individual Entry**

- **Description**: Fees per person for entering the park, often applicable for pedestrians, cyclists, or hikers.
- **Examples**: Range from $3 to $15 per person, with discounts for seniors, veterans, and children.

Special Permits
1. **Camping Permits**

- **Description**: Required for overnight stays in campgrounds or backcountry areas.
- **Cost**: Varies widely based on amenities, location, and seasonality.

2. **Special Use Permits**

- **Description**: Needed for organized events, commercial filming, or large group gatherings within parks.
- **Application Process**: Requires advance planning and approval from park authorities.

Purchasing and Policies

- **Online Reservations**: Many parks offer online purchasing options for passes and permits, facilitating convenience and planning.
- **Discount Programs**: Senior discounts, military discounts,

and annual passes for veterans may be available, promoting accessibility and inclusivity.
- **Revenue Allocation**: Fees support park maintenance, conservation efforts, visitor services, and educational programs, ensuring sustainable park management.

Visitor Tips

- **Plan Ahead**: Research park fees and pass options in advance, particularly for popular parks during peak seasons.
- **Fee Waivers**: Some parks offer fee-free days or waivers for certain groups, encouraging visitation and public engagement.
- **Leave No Trace**: Respect park regulations, pack out trash, and adhere to fire restrictions to preserve natural environments.

Understanding park passes and fees allows visitors to budget effectively, support conservation efforts, and enjoy recreational activities responsibly while exploring the natural wonders of parks across the country.

Accessibility Information

Accessibility information ensures that parks and recreational areas are inclusive and accessible to all individuals, including those with disabilities or special needs. Here's a detailed overview of accessibility information for parks:

Accessibility Features

1. Accessible Parking

- **Description**: Designated parking spaces close to park entrances and facilities for visitors with disabilities.
- **Features**: Wide parking spaces, accessible pathways to amenities.

2. Accessible Trails and Pathways

- **Description**: Paved or compacted trails suitable for wheelchairs, strollers, or mobility devices.
- **Features**: Gentle slopes, handrails, and clear signage for navigation.

3. Accessible Facilities

- **Description**: Accessible restrooms, visitor centers, picnic areas, and campsites.
- **Features**: Wide entrances, accessible counters, grab bars, and designated parking.

4. Assistive Listening Devices

- **Description**: Available for ranger-led programs or multimedia presentations.
- **Features**: Enhances auditory experiences for visitors with hearing impairments.

5. Accessible Programs and Services

- **Description**: Inclusive interpretive programs, guided tours, and recreational activities.
- **Features**: Trained staff, adaptive equipment, and modified activities.

Accessibility Resources
1. Accessibility Guides

- **Description**: Online or printed guides detailing accessible features, services, and contact information.
- **Availability**: Provided by park websites, visitor centers, or upon request.

2. Accessibility Maps

- **Description**: Detailed maps highlighting accessible trails, facilities, and parking areas.
- **Features**: Clear symbols and legends for ease of use.

3. Service Animal Policy

- **Description**: Guidelines for bringing service animals into parks.
- **Features**: Information on permissible areas and responsibilities of pet owners.

Accessibility Initiatives
1. Universal Design

- **Description**: Incorporation of universal design principles in park infrastructure and amenities.

- **Benefits**: Enhances usability for individuals of all abilities without special adaptations.

2. **Collaborations and Feedback**

- **Description**: Partnerships with disability advocacy groups and community feedback mechanisms.
- **Benefits**: Continuous improvement of accessibility features based on visitor input and evolving standards.

Visitor Tips

- **Advance Planning**: Review accessibility information and contact park staff for specific needs or accommodations.
- **Equipment Rental**: Some parks offer adaptive equipment rentals for activities like kayaking or hiking.
- **Etiquette**: Respect designated accessible spaces and facilities, ensuring they remain available for those who need them.

Accessibility information ensures that parks are welcoming environments where all visitors can enjoy nature, recreational activities, and educational opportunities. By providing comprehensive accessibility features, resources, and initiatives, parks promote inclusivity and enhance the overall visitor experience for individuals of diverse abilities.

Safety Tips and Regulations

Safety tips and regulations are essential for ensuring the well-being of visitors and preserving the natural environment in parks and recreational areas. Here's a detailed overview:

Safety Tips
  1. **Plan and Prepare**

- **Research**: Familiarize yourself with park rules, regulations, and potential hazards before your visit.
- **Weather**: Check weather forecasts and plan activities accordingly to avoid inclement weather.
- **Route**: Plan hiking or biking routes, noting distances, terrain, and estimated time.

2. **Stay on Designated Trails**

- **Trail Markings**: Follow marked trails to avoid getting lost or damaging fragile ecosystems.
- **Wildlife**: Respect wildlife and observe from a safe distance; never approach or feed animals.

3. **Water Safety**

- **Swimming**: Swim only in designated areas with lifeguards present, if available.
- **Boating**: Wear life jackets, follow boating regulations, and be aware of water conditions.

4. **Campfire Safety**

- **Permits**: Obtain necessary permits for campfires and follow regulations for fire management.
- **Extinguishing**: Completely extinguish campfires with water, ensuring they are cold to the touch before leaving.

5. **First Aid and Emergency Preparedness**

- **Kit**: Carry a first aid kit with essential supplies for minor injuries and emergencies.
- **Communication**: Have a charged cell phone, emergency contacts, and knowledge of park emergency procedures.

Regulations
1. **Park Rules**

- **Pets**: Follow pet regulations, keeping them leashed and under control at all times.
- **Litter**: Pack out all trash and dispose of waste properly to preserve the environment.
- **Noise**: Respect quiet hours and noise restrictions to minimize disturbance to wildlife and other visitors.

2. **Permits and Fees**

- **Entry**: Pay applicable entry fees or obtain permits for specific activities such as camping or backcountry hiking.
- **Special Use**: Obtain permits for special events, commercial filming, or large group gatherings.

Environmental Considerations
1. **Leave No Trace Principles**

- **Pack It In, Pack It Out**: Carry out all trash and leave natural areas as you found them.
- **Minimize Impact**: Stay on trails, avoid trampling vegetation, and respect natural habitats.

2. **Wildlife Conservation**

- **Observation**: Observe wildlife from a safe distance to prevent stress or harm to animals.
- **Feeding**: Never feed wildlife as it can alter natural behaviors and endanger both animals and humans.

Visitor Tips

- **Educate Yourself**: Attend ranger programs or interpretive exhibits to learn about park history, wildlife, and conservation efforts.
- **Stay Informed**: Check park websites, visitor centers, or local ranger stations for updated safety information and alerts.
- **Group Safety**: Travel in groups when possible, especially in remote areas, and inform others of your plans and expected return times.

Safety tips and regulations in parks ensure a safe and enjoyable experience for visitors while promoting conservation and environmental stewardship. By following guidelines, respecting wildlife, and being prepared for emergencies, visitors contribute to the preservation of natural resources and enhance their own exploration of parks and recreational areas.

Packing Lists and Gear Recommendations.

Creating a packing list and choosing the right gear are crucial steps to ensure comfort, safety, and enjoyment during outdoor adventures in parks and recreational areas. Here's a detailed guide to packing lists and gear recommendations:

Packing List
1. **Clothing**

- **Layering**: Base layers (moisture-wicking), insulating layers (fleece or down jackets), waterproof outer layers (jacket and pants).
- **Footwear**: Sturdy hiking boots or shoes with good traction, comfortable socks (wool or synthetic), water shoes for water activities.
- **Headwear**: Sun hat or cap, beanie or hat for warmth, sunglasses with UV protection.
- **Accessories**: Gloves or mittens, scarf or neck gaiter for cold weather, swimwear for water activities.

2. **Gear and Equipment**

- **Backpack**: Lightweight and durable, with enough capacity for essentials and hydration system compatibility.
- **Navigation**: Map, compass, or GPS device, and trail guidebooks for navigation.
- **Lighting**: Headlamp or flashlight with extra batteries for night hikes or emergencies.
- **Trekking Poles**: Adjustable and collapsible poles for stability on uneven terrain.

3. Camping Essentials

- **Tent**: Lightweight and weatherproof tent suitable for the number of occupants.
- **Sleeping Gear**: Sleeping bag (appropriate temperature rating), sleeping pad for insulation and comfort.
- **Cooking Gear**: Stove (camp stove or backpacking stove), cookware (pot, pan, utensils), and fuel.
- **Food and Water**: Non-perishable food items, snacks, water bottles or hydration reservoirs, water purification system.

4. Personal Items

- **First Aid Kit**: Basic supplies for treating minor injuries, medications, insect repellent, sunscreen.
- **Toiletries**: Toilet paper, hand sanitizer, biodegradable soap, toothbrush and toothpaste.
- **Personal Identification**: ID, permits, and emergency contact information.

Gear Recommendations
1. Backpack

- **Type**: Consider a backpack with adjustable straps, padded hip belt, and multiple compartments for organization.
- **Capacity**: Choose a size based on trip length and gear volume (e.g., 30-50 liters for day hikes, 50-70 liters for overnight trips).

2. Footwear

- **Hiking Boots**: Waterproof, ankle support, and grippy soles for traction on varied terrain.
- **Water Shoes**: Lightweight, quick-drying shoes for water activities like kayaking or river crossings.

3. Navigation

- **GPS Device**: Handheld GPS units with preloaded maps and waypoint capabilities.
- **Map and Compass**: Waterproof maps and a reliable compass for navigation in remote areas.

4. Tent and Sleeping Gear

- **Tent**: Lightweight and easy to set up, with weather resistance and adequate ventilation.
- **Sleeping Bag**: Down or synthetic insulation, suitable for expected temperatures, and compressible for packing.

5. Cooking and Hydration

- **Stove**: Compact and efficient stove system with fuel efficiency for extended trips.
- **Cookware**: Lightweight pots and pans with heat-resistant handles and lids for cooking versatility.

Additional Tips

- **Weather Considerations**: Pack clothing and gear suitable for expected weather conditions, including rain gear and extra layers for cold nights.

- **Weight Distribution**: Distribute weight evenly in your backpack to maintain balance and comfort during hiking.
- **Trial Runs**: Test new gear and equipment before the trip to ensure functionality and familiarity.

By preparing a comprehensive packing list and selecting appropriate gear, outdoor enthusiasts can optimize their experiences in parks and recreational areas. Prioritize comfort, safety, and environmental stewardship by choosing gear that meets your needs and conditions while respecting natural surroundings. Planning ahead and packing smartly enhances enjoyment and ensures readiness for various outdoor activities and adventures.

8

Conclusion

In conclusion, this book serves as an indispensable companion for anyone eager to explore the diverse and captivating landscapes of Florida's state parks. From the tranquil springs and lush forests of Northern Florida to the vibrant coastal vistas and historical sites of Southern and Coastal Florida, each chapter provides detailed insights, practical tips, and rich narratives that invite readers to embark on unforgettable outdoor adventures.

Throughout these pages, you'll find comprehensive guides on park amenities, accommodation options, local flora and fauna, and a myriad of recreational activities, ensuring that every visit is both enriching and well-prepared. Whether you're planning a family camping trip, seeking secluded hiking trails, or simply yearning to immerse yourself in the natural beauty of Florida, this book equips you with the knowledge and resources needed to make the most of your journey.

Beyond practical advice, this book celebrates the cultural her-

CONCLUSION

itage, conservation efforts, and unique experiences that define each park, encouraging readers to appreciate and protect these natural treasures for generations to come. With detailed maps, insightful narratives, and a passion for exploration, it is our hope that this guide inspires you to discover and connect with the unparalleled beauty of Florida's state parks, fostering a deep appreciation for the outdoors and a sense of wonder in every adventure.